Dog Parenting

How to Have an Outrageously Happy, Well-Adjusted Canine

Andrea Rains Waggener
with Patti Schaefer, D.V.M.

Adams Media
Avon, Massachusetts

Published by Adams Media, an F+W Publications Company
57 Littlefield Street, Avon, MA 02322 U.S.A.
www.adamsmedia.com

ISBN: 1-59337-492-5

Printed in Canada.

J I H G F E D C B A

Library of Congress Cataloging-in-Publication Data
Waggener, Andrea Rains
Dog parenting : how to have an outrageously happy, well-adjusted canine /
by Andrea Rains Waggener, with Patti Schaefer.
p. cm.
ISBN 1-59337-492-5
1. Dogs. I. Schaefer, Patti. II. Title.

SF427.W12 2006
636.7'0887--dc22
                         2005029893

This publication is designed to provide accurate and authoritative information with
regard to the subject matter covered. It is sold with the understanding that the publisher
is not engaged in rendering legal, accounting, or other professional advice. If legal advice
or other expert assistance is required, the services of a competent professional person
should be sought.
—From a *Declaration of Principles* jointly adopted by a Committee of the American Bar
Association and a Committee of Publishers and Associations

Many of the designations used by manufacturers and sellers to distinguish their products
are claimed as trademarks. Where those designations appear in this book and Adams
Media was aware of a trademark claim, the designations have been printed with initial
capital letters.

This book is available at quantity discounts for bulk purchases.
For information, please call 1-800-872-5627.

Dedication

For Mom and Dad, who share with me a love of dogs, who bought me my first dog, and who learned, along with me, how to be great dog parents.

And for Dizzy and Muggins, who have made being a dog mom one of the most rewarding parts of my life.

Contents

Part I: FUN   1

Part II: COMFORT   65

Part III: SECURITY   119

Part IV: LOVE   173

Acknowledgments

Thank you to Muggins, who fills my life with joy. A big thank you to my husband, Tim, for being a great dog dad and for being my reader and steadfast supporter. Thanks also to my parents for being great dog-grandparents and for believing in me. Thank you to all my friends with dogs—you and your furry kids have so enriched my life. I owe special thanks to Michael Baldwin, who encouraged me to write this book—he told me that I should write what I'm passionate about, and there's little I'm more passionate about than being a dog parent. Thank you to my agent, Alison Picard, for seeing the potential in the manuscript and finding the perfect home for it. Thank you to my editor, Kate Epstein, for her vision of what this book could be and for her clear instructions that helped me write that book. And last, but not least, thank you to all dogs, who put up with us troublesome humans and give us more love than we could possibly ever give back.

Introduction
by Patti Schaefer, D.V.M.

"My dogs are my children." "These are my babies." "My spouse and I decided not to have children, so our dogs are our kids."

I hear these statements often in my practice. It's a feeling I share with my clients, as my dogs are my children too. My world revolves around my dogs.

While in school, I had the privilege of working with the late Dr. Leo Bustad, a pioneer in studying the human/animal bond. Much has been written on the importance of this bond and its positive effects on our lives. The pet industry has grown into a multibillion-dollar industry that includes health care, toys, food, grooming supplies, doggy day-care centers, and training schools. I have known people who set up their households to accommodate their dogs or who even sold a house that wasn't a good match for dogs. Recently, while reading one of my veterinary journals, an article made reference to veterinary medicine as "family" medicine. Some states have even adopted the word "guardian" to replace "owner" in legal language.

I am fortunate in my practice to have a clientele that considers their dogs a part of the family. One of my clients and her service dog share a strong bond. He is the reason she gets up in the morning; he gives her a reason to live, to care for him. Another strong bond I see in my practice is the team relationship between canine athlete and handler. To be successful, both have to be of one mind. This requires countless hours learning each other, and that means reading the language of body and mind.

The first time Ande and Tim came into my office with Muggins, I could feel their concern for her. She had been seen by other veterinarians but was still having some uncontrolled gastrointestinal problems. We talked for quite a while about the situation. I examined Muggins, treated her, and made suggestions for her care. I knew that Muggins was their baby.

What is easy to forget is that this relationship is a two-way street. If our dogs are our children, then we are dog parents. In this book, Ande describes personal experiences of what it takes to be a good dog parent. Her perspective is multidimensional, seeing life from both sides in order to create the happiest and healthiest environment possible.

Dogs give us so much. Ande shows us how to give back by strengthening and enhancing the bond between dog parent and dog. Please join her in this revolution.

Introduction
A Cold, Wet Nose

"A dog is like an eternal Peter Pan, a child who never grows old and who therefore is always available to love and be loved."

—Aaron Katcher, American educator and writer

Dogs. Furry and four-legged, with wet noses, wagging tails, and loving eyes—dogs are one of the greatest blessings in life.

I have always loved dogs. I bugged my mom and stepdad incessantly until they got me one when I was seven years old. When my parents finally took me to a pet store and let me visit the puppies in a flimsy chicken-wire and wood-frame enclosure, Shorty was the one who came from the back of the pack and trotted directly to me. Shorty was an all-American half-cocker, half-beagle with a head too small for her body and freckles everywhere. She wagged her tail and licked my fingers. I was in love.

"Can I have this one?" I pleaded with my parents, expecting the usual negative response.

But they said yes. No child could have been happier when I picked up that little puppy (who seemed huge to me), draped her over my shoulder, and paraded her through the store so everyone could see us. I finally had a dog, and I wanted the whole world to know it.

Shorty was fifteen years old when she died during my senior year of college. My parents and I have lived with guilt over Shorty's life ever since she left us. We treated Shorty like a dog. She slept in the basement at night, wasn't allowed on most of the furniture, was walked only once in a while—when the spirit moved us—and was frequently tied up in the backyard. We thought nothing of leaving her in a kennel. We loved her, of course, and we gave her toys and cuddled her. We celebrated her birthday and included her in most of our family outings. We were good dog owners. But we didn't know anything about being dog *parents*.

In my life, I have spent only short periods without a dog—during the months I was away at school, for instance, and for one year after college. During that time, I had dog radar. Whenever I saw a dog, I'd virtually run over the dog's owner to get a chance to pet the dog. I wanted just a touch of fur, a quick lick, a second or two of looking into sweet doggy eyes. I needed a regular canine fix.

I'd been married for a year when Brad, my husband at the time, and I got Dizzy, a blonde cocker spaniel. Dizzy was a little on the grumpy side and had a myriad of health problems, but I adored her. It used to be our joke that if Brad and Dizzy were drowning, and I could only save one of them, I would save Brad only because he earned such great money. It wasn't much of a joke, and it wasn't true, either. I probably would have saved Diz.

Dizzy was only nine years old when she died suddenly of liver disease—one day she was fine, and three weeks later, she was gone. I had never known such grief. I felt like my life had been wrenched away, and no one understood. According to the rest of the world, she was, after all, just a dog. But everyone was wrong. She was my child.

We brought Muggins home less than a week after Dizzy died. It seemed like a good idea at the time. A new puppy would get my mind off losing Dizzy, my parents and friends told me. Brad wasn't gung ho about getting another dog so quickly, but he went along with it.

Muggins is a springer spaniel, and true to her breed, she's exuberant, energetic, and endlessly eager for action. Like all puppies, she had no off switch. She would play for hours and want more. She usually played at driving mommy crazy. There were days when I would happily have given her to any passing stranger.

Those days passed, though, and soon, I wouldn't have traded her for any amount of money. I'd shared an amazing bond with Dizzy, but the bond between me and Muggins was even stronger. Perhaps this was because I spent more time with Muggins. I quit my career in law a couple years before Dizzy died. She had to endure six years of being left alone when I was in law school and later when I worked. But I was home most of the day with Muggins. She was my shadow. One woman called Muggins my "Velcro dog"— she's attached to me and I to her.

Even though I began to learn about dog parenting with Dizzy, I was still a novice when she died. My time with Muggins is what has turned me into a great dog mom. Some people tell me Muggins is spoiled. If so, spoiled is what all dogs should be. Muggins is an ourtrageously happy dog, and I'm an ourtrageously happy dog mom. We have a relationship that enriches and nurtures us both. After nine years of giving Muggins the best life I possibly can, I consider myself an expert at raising an ourtrageously happy canine.

A few years ago, after Brad and I divorced and I had been living alone for a few years, I met Tim, a wonderful man who is now my husband. One of the aspects of Tim that stole my heart was his dog parenting skills. He fell in love with Muggins and threw himself wholeheartedly into the role of dog dad. She's crazy about her new daddy because he spoils her as much, or more, than I do.

Roger Caras, author of *A Dog is Listening,* says, "Dogs are children that are never quite able to grow up, no matter how smart they are." Jeffrey Moussaieff Masson, author of *Dogs Never Lie About Love,* agrees. He says "dogs remain permanent juveniles, with us *in loco parentis.*" He asks, "If we are the 'parents' of a dog, what are our teaching responsibilities? How much should we attempt to make a dog fit into the human world and how much can we allow a dog to be a dog?" Throughout his book, Masson avoids using the word "owner" to refer to people's relationship with dogs; Masson doesn't believe a dog is "a thing that we can own and dispose of at will, giving it away, abandoning it, or even having it killed when we move from one city to another."

I know the difference between being a mere dog owner and a dog parent, and I'm familiar with the little extras that make the difference between a good dog parent and a great one. If you don't believe me, ask Muggins. She'll "Arroo!" and wag her tail. You can interpret that however you'd like.

A caveat before I go any further. This is a book about dog parenting—literally, providing nurturing and love to a dog similar to what one would provide a child. In discussing how to be a great dog parent, I often draw parallels to the parenting of human children. Lest I offend any parents of kids out there, I do acknowledge that a dog is not a human. Therefore, parenting a dog is obviously different in many respects from parenting a child. But we have to start somewhere when we're learning a new skill. Most people can relate to how one might parent a child, so the comparison serves as a useful reference point.

Before we proceed, here's a note. Because I believe that we have an obligation to raise canines as if they were little, furry people, I dislike referring to dogs as "it." To avoid the wordiness that comes with "he or she," when I refer to a singular dog, I will use "she" or "her."

Okay, so I know most people love their dogs and want to provide them with a great life. Not everyone, however, knows how to truly and completely spoil a canine. That's what this book is about.

This book does *not* describe how to housetrain your dog or teach her to sit, stay, come, or heel. We need to know how to train these behaviors, of course, because dogs do need *some* training, just as children need direction. If you want a happy canine, one that you and other people will enjoy so much that you'll lavish attention on the dog, you need to give your dog at least the basics in good manners. All dogs need to be housetrained and need to learn to sit, stay, and come. Other commands are useful too. But this book goes beyond this kind of simple training.

It focuses on a dog's need to live a happy life, expressing her personality naturally and fully. To give your dog this kind of freedom, you need to be a dog parent, not a dog owner. This book is intended to go where other dog-training and obedience books will never go. It will teach you how to spoil your dog—how to *raise* a happy and healthy dog.

It doesn't take much, actually. If you love your dog, and I mean really *love* your dog, much of great dog parenting will come naturally to you. The job requires four essentials. To be a great dog parent, you need to provide your dog with fun, comfort, security, and love. This book gives you ideas for providing these essentials in buckets. Of course, not everyone has the life circumstances to follow all of the advice in this book. But if you can begin incorporating even some of the suggestions into your life with your dog, you can pat yourself on the back and scratch your dog on the butt because you will be a great dog parent, and you will have an outrageously happy canine.

PART I: FUN

Most kids know how to have fun. Unfortunately, when we grow up, in the struggle to be responsible, productive adults, we often forget that basic skill. If you need to relearn how to have fun, you can watch kids. Or you can watch a happy dog.

Dogs were born to have fun. It's one of the things they do best. To be a great dog parent, you must be able to nurture your dog's desire for all things fun. Though this may sound easy, it isn't quite as simple as you might think. Throwing a ball and taking your dog for regular walks, for example, is a good start. But great dog parents do much more.

Instead of forcing your dog to adjust to your needs, as a great dog parent, you must adjust your lifestyle to work with your dog's personality and to the way your dog wants to play. Instead of buying just a few toys, you buy so many that your dog could get lost in the toy basket. You allow your dog time to run free and off her leash. You walk your dog in practically any weather. You let your dog get dirty. You make sure your dog can always see outside to watch the world go by. You do more than just let your dog ride in the car—you make travel with your dog fun and interactive. You celebrate your dog's birthday and include her in other celebrations.

Honey Loring, owner of Camp Gone to the Dogs, says, "Fun is the name of the game. If your dog's tail isn't up [you're] doing something wrong." Great dog parents know the importance of making life for their dog fun. You also know that the bonus for making life fun for your dog is that it makes life fun for you, too.

chapter 1

Encouraging Your Dog's Natural Interests

Good parents let their kids be themselves. They encourage whatever interests and nurture whatever talents their children have. If their kid excels at computer games and playing the xylophone, good parents will take the child to the local computer game club and buy the best xylophone they can find—even if they'd rather see the kid play Little League and tickle the ivories of a piano. Good parents find activities that allow their kids to use their natural abilities and express their natural passions. Like children, dogs have interests, talents, and passions that are unique to them; therefore, part of being a good *dog* parent requires this kind of encouragement and nurturing.

You Are What You're Bred to Be

Most dogs were bred for some specific task. Even mixed breeds have a heritage that makes them more interested in some activities and less interested in others. For example, retrievers obviously retrieve. Herding dogs herd. Hunting dogs hunt. Terriers were bred to burrow into small places and catch rodents, so they dig. Greyhounds were bred for speed; they love to run fast. Labradors and spaniels love the water. Scent hounds love to track. Some dogs were bred for looks and are best suited for lying around prettily and eating doggy bonbons. One thing you can count on is that no matter what kind of dog you have, she *will* have a natural inclination toward some activity or other.

When I say you need to allow your dog to express her natural tendencies, I'm not talking about all dogs' natural inclination to investigate smelly things and roll in poop or on dead things. I'm talking about your dog's instincts to perform some kind of job. Every dog has such an instinct. The key to a happy dog (and a happy you) is to allow your dog to find a way to express those natural instincts. That's what a good dog parent does.

Discovering Your True Colors

How can you discover your dog's natural inclination?

A little bit of observation is a good start. Watching your dog at play and watching your dog interact with other dogs will give you an idea about her natural tendencies.

If your dog isn't giving you enough clues, you can do some research. Go online and start investigating breeds. The American Kennel Club has a great Web site, at *www. akc.org*, where breeds are listed in alphabetical order. Click on any breed name, and you'll get a full description of the breed, which will tell you what that breed commonly likes to do. There are hundreds of other breed-specific Web sites online as well. Most breeds also have entire books devoted to them. Check out your library or local bookstore.

What if your dog is a mixed breed and you're not sure what to look up? Your vet can help you there. Most veterinarians can offer pretty accurate opinions of what breeds went into your dog's mix. Once you know the mix, look up all those breeds, and then watch your dog to see which breed's tendencies predominate.

If you're thinking of getting a new dog, consider the dog's tendencies *before* you get her. Books that offer advice on choosing the right dog suggest that you should be aware of what the particular breed you're considering is inclined to do. Some people who want a docile companion end up with dogs that are very active. When the dog won't settle down, she ends up in a shelter. Some people who want an active dog, on the other hand, end up with a couch canine. It's a good idea to know what you're getting. Unlike the case with human children, to some extent you can choose a canine child whose qualities fit your lifestyle.

There's More Than One Way to Skin a Cat

Now don't panic. Making sure your dog gets to do his or her natural job doesn't mean you have to totally disrupt your life. It doesn't mean that if you have a herding dog, you have to own a sheep farm. If you have a terrier, you don't need to be surrounded by rats. And if you have a hunting dog, you don't need to tramp out into the woods and shoot wildlife.

Muggins, being a springer spaniel, is a hunting dog. I got her from a breeder who bred springers specifically for sport, that is, for hunting. Muggins, consequently, has a strong hunting instinct. I, however, don't hunt. I'm a vegetarian. I don't even hunt for hamburgers at fast-food joints.

When Muggins was a puppy, I took her to a park with fields of tall grass. One day, Muggins flushed a pheasant. The bird fluttered up into the air, and Muggins sprang out of the grass after it, looking toward me with an expression of delighted expectation. Her communication was clear: "Well, Mom, shoot it." When I didn't shoot the bird, she looked a bit confused. But not for long. Still pleased with herself, she returned to bounding through the tall grass with her tail furiously a-wag.

Muggins flushed several pheasants and chased countless ducks and geese before apparently reaching the conclusion that I wasn't going to cooperate in her bird-hunting projects. So she took up a new activity—insect hunting.

It began quite by accident. On a warm summer evening when the back door was open, a large crane fly flew into the house and fluttered up the wall of the family room. Muggins spotted the thing and charged across the room. Her gaze fixed intently on the bug, she assumed the most beautiful and classic pointing stance I'd ever seen. Body elongated, tail straight out and rigid, ears pricked, front paw lifted off the ground, she zeroed in on that crane fly, and looked at me. Of course, I knew what she wanted.

I may not be willing to kill a bird. But I don't have a problem doing away with a crane fly. So while Muggins quivered with excitement and whined her enthusiasm, I went to get the flyswatter. Muggins watched with interest and increasing excitement as I stalked the bug. When it flew away from me, she'd tremble and whine. When I'd get close to it, she'd bark, louder and louder the closer I got. It was a canine version of hotter/colder. When I finally cornered the insect and smacked it with the flyswatter, Muggins was in a frenzy.

The bug fell off the wall and landed on the floor. Muggins pounced on it . . . and ate it. Not exactly what I had in mind. But it didn't seem to hurt her.

From that point, Muggins's mission was clear—to seek out and corner all insects, to boldly do what no other springer had done before. Muggins soon learned that dark spots on walls are often insects. She found spiders and mosquitoes and flies, oh my. Every time I killed one, she whirled in circles of ecstasy, immensely and inordinately proud of herself.

She found them. I killed them. Every time I killed a bug Muggins found, I rewarded her with a treat. Thus encouraged, Muggins took to lying on the top of the back of the sofa scanning the walls and the ceiling for prey.

This is an example of how you can help your dog be what she was meant to be without changing your entire lifestyle. You need to get creative.

Getting Creative

I have a friend who has a mixed-breed dog named Lucy. Lucy is half retriever and half Australian shepherd. My friend has found a way to satisfy both of Lucy's natural instincts. First, whenever she walks, my friend takes along a Frisbee or ball and throws it ahead of Lucy as they go. This satisfies the retriever half.

Second, every few weeks or so, she takes Lucy to a special place in a rural area an hour or so from where she lives. It's a place that's set up to let dogs herd. Some ingenious person got a group of docile and even-tempered sheep and set up a business. People bring their herding dogs to practice herding sheep. Some people who train their dogs for competition use the place to perfect their dogs' skills. Some people, like my friend, visit the place just because they want to give their herding dog the experience of doing what the dog was bred to do.

Once you find out what your dog was bred for, do a little brainstorming about how you can help your dog have the fun he or she was meant to have. If your dog is a scent hound, for instance, perhaps you could hide bones for her in your yard. If your dog likes to dig, maybe you could take her to a beach or a sandbox (as long as there are no kids in it), and bury a toy for her to discover. If your dog wants to fetch, be sure you spend a lot of time throwing balls. If your dog wants to hunt, let your dog hunt—even if it's just insects.

Hi Ho, Hi Ho, It's Off to Work We Go

Allowing your dog to do what she was meant to do makes her a better dog because it gives her a sense of purpose. A dog that has a purpose, however contrived, is a happier, more contented dog. A more contented dog is a dog that is more pleasant to be around.

Obviously, dogs need outlets for their energy. They also need to feel useful. I'm sure you've noticed the zeal with which most dogs protect their property. They love watching for strangers and alerting the household to any approaching entity. They love it because they're doing their job, and they know it.

Dogs in the wild have a role to play in the pack. Dogs in your households play a role as well. We see them as companions and think their simple presence in our family is enough. But they need more. They need work. It may not seem like work to you, but your dog's activities are your dog's work. Make sure your dog is doing work she loves.

I Want to Play My Way

When your dog isn't working, she's playing.Some parents would like their kids to be athletes and are disappointed if they turn out to be chess champions instead. Some parents want kids with musical talent and are disappointed if their child doesn't know a treble clef from a cleft palate. But a good parent shows interest and support for whatever a child loves. The same is true of good dog parents.

It's All Your Fault

When it comes to play, Muggins likes to be chased, thanks to my dear ex-husband. When Muggins was a puppy, Brad enjoyed racing around the house with her, chasing her through the house with a lot of whoops and yodels. Muggins loved it.

Muggins's ears would prick up whenever Brad made a move. She'd drop into the doggy play position, front end down, back end up in the air, and she'd race to find a toy. Any toy. It didn't matter what she had. In fact, nothing at all would be okay in a pinch. Usually, though, she'd grab something, tuck in her back end and take off like a mad rabbit with Brad right on her tail.

This was a riot to watch, and I didn't discourage it. He was happy. She was happy. I got to sit on the sofa and be amused. Until the divorce. Then I had a little problem. Muggins likes to be chased, and I don't much like chasing.

Let this be a lesson. Some of your dog's play tendencies will be inborn. Some of your dog's play preferences, however, will result from what your dog becomes used to. What is cute when your dog is a puppy may not be so cute when your dog grows up. When you first get your dog, you need to establish play routines that you and your dog are both going to be happy with for the duration of your dog's life.

You Made Your Bed

But what do you do if your dog already has a way of playing that you're not crazy about?

Basically, you just deal with it. Good dog parents make sacrifices.

Muggins, like all dogs, needs exercise, lots of it, and I'm happy to take her on long walks. I'm just not real big on tearing around my living room chasing a dog that's only trotting at half speed while I'm running full out and huffing like a steam engine doing my best to catch her. I'm especially not real keen on it when she decides that the best time for this delightful activity is right after I've eaten dinner or just after I've settled in under the afghan to relax after a busy day.

But, hey, Muggins is my dog, and she likes to play the way she likes to play. It's part of her personality, and it's my job as her dog mom, to accommodate her, at least once in awhile. If you have a dog that likes to be chased, I've learned a couple tricks to make things easier.

First, you don't need to run flat out after your dog if you act like you're some sort of deranged monster, raising your arms and flapping them around as you march after her. Your dog will get enough of a kick out of this that it will keep her trotting in a circle without much effort on your part.

An even better trick is to chase your dog once around the living room and then start whooping like a car alarm or a warrior heading into battle: Aei yi yi yi yi! That will really get your dog going. If you're lucky, you may be able to get your dog running in circles all by herself. All you have to do is keep whooping and goose her on the rump every time she goes by.

If you inadvertently create a play situation that suits your dog but doesn't suit you, do what you can to make it more enjoyable for you while still giving your dog the fun she wants. The happier you are, the happier your dog will be.

If It's Fun, Go for It

Thankfully, I've found other ways to play besides the run-and-chase that Muggins loves. For instance, she likes to chase bubbles. One afternoon, I was in the backyard idly blowing bubbles. I like bubbles. They're a great way to get in touch with your inner child. I discovered they're also a fine way to lazily entertain your dog.

Muggins chased bubbles the first time she saw them. She had so much fun that I began blowing bubbles just for her. Now when I get out the container of bubble solution, she whirls in circles and begins a frenzy of barking. She doesn't stop barking until I start blowing.

Some dogs like to wrestle. Muggins doesn't. But she does sometimes enjoy attacking my feet when they're under the covers. She likes for me to wiggle my feet around so she can pounce on them and bite at the blankets covering them. Hey, whatever wags her tail! I'm game.

Every dog has a favorite way of playing. Dizzy liked tug-a-war. It was her favorite way to play, and most of her toys were tug toys. Shorty loved balloons. She'd watch intently as you blew up a balloon, and then, when you batted it up in the air, she'd bop it repeatedly with her nose to keep it up there.

Some dog owners, like some parents of human kids, seem to think their dog should play a certain way. If you have a dog with behavior problems, or if you're training a dog for high levels of competition, canine behaviorists suggest controlling your dog's type of play. If the dog doesn't play in a certain way, the dog doesn't get to play. However, the average dog doesn't need that kind of rigid control.

You need to learn to accommodate your dog and play the way your dog wants to play. Remember, the point of play is to have fun. So let your dog lead the way here. As long as it's not destructive, let your dog choose the way he or she wants to play. Be willing to try something you've never done before.

If you're feeling lazy, see if your dog will chase a flashlight beam in a dark room. Find out if your dog likes to watch television, which can make for great playtime for a dog. Get one of those battery-operated balls that rolls around by itself, and see if your dog likes chasing it. You can also try toys that are meant to hold kibble or treats. Any pet store or catalog will have them. The toys are usually rubber, and you put kibble or treats inside. The dog rolls it around to get the food out. Experiment with all kinds of play and find the play that makes your dog happy.

Happy, busy dogs, as I've said, as a general rule, are not annoying or destructive dogs. In that way, being a good dog parent and playing the way your dog wants to play is good for some peace of mind. I suppose a little racing around the living room shrieking like an idiot is a small price to pay for that.

Don't Just Love Me, Accept Me

Dog parents accept their dogs. Laurence Sheehan, author of *Living With Dogs*, explains how acceptance becomes easier when you understand your dog's breed, its natural instincts. Sheehan learned more about his dog's breed, the English setter, and the knowledge, as he puts it, "made it easier to accept [his dog] for what he was—an animal with attention deficit disorder by day, a lovesick couch potato by night."

It's great fun to discover your dog's interests and find her natural role. When you can allow dogs to be themselves as much as possible, you'll not only have a good dog, you'll be a good dog parent.

chapter 2

Giving Your Dog Lots of Toys

I'm sure you've seen the bumper sticker, "He who dies with the most toys wins." The plates refer to humans and their "toys." But if dogs drove cars, no doubt this bumper sticker would be quite popular.

Toys, Glorious Toys

Dogs love toys. Old toys. New toys. Expensive toys. Hand-me down toys. Even toys that aren't toys—Kleenex boxes, paper towel tubes, paper bags. You need to provide your dog with plenty of toys—the more the better. Almost every time I go to a pet store to buy pet supplies, I buy Muggins a new toy. Muggins *loves* getting new toys.

Does she need new toys?

Certainly not. She has more toys than she could ever play with. Muggins has a pile of toys nearly two feet tall. A few years ago, I bought a large basket, a foot and a half in diameter, to hold Muggins's toys. The basket is now overflowing, and toys are piled around the edges of the basket.

Most of Muggins's toys sit in the bottom of her basket and never get hauled out. Once in awhile, she digs down in the basket and pulls out a toy she hasn't played with in awhile. She comes prancing in with a rope, a pull toy, or a squeaky toy that I haven't seen in a long time and drops it proudly in my lap. "Oh, a rope toy," I say in an enthusiastic, high-pitched voice. (See Chapter 30 for more information about baby talking to your dog.) "You brought me a rope toy!" She wags her tail and smiles a broad doggy smile.

Muggins loves plush toys the best. She has a couple dozen of them—a stuffed frog, a tiger, a bear, a duck, a horse, a spider, a crab, a rat. . . . All manner of plush critters that squeak, grunt, and rattle when Muggins carries them around. She also enjoys her plastic squeaky toys, rope toys, and my old socks.

If you want to be a great dog parent, you need to give your dog lots of toys. Lots and lots of toys. The winner of the 2005 Westminster Kennel Club Dog Show, a German shorthaired pointer named Carlee, reportedly has over 200 squeaky toys that she loves to sleep with. She obviously has a great dog parent.

You Can Play With Anything

Maybe you don't have the money to buy your dog 200 squeaky toys. That's okay. Dogs aren't picky when it comes to toys.

I've given Muggins socks since she was a puppy. I've heard all the conventional wisdom about socks. If you give your dog socks, the books say, your dog won't know that it's wrong to play with *your* socks and you'll find yourself missing socks. But socks are great dog toys. A pair of socks knotted together makes a perfect tug toy, and every dog I've ever known loves to toss around socks, pounce on them, and shake them until the sock is well and truly "dead."

So when I wear out a pair of socks, I wash them, knot them together, and give them to Muggins for a toy. And she never, ever takes *my* socks. It amazes me that I never had to teach her the difference. She just seems to know.

Socks make great toys. In fact, many top trainers of performance dogs use socks to teach dogs how to play. Not all dogs play with toys naturally. Trainers put food in a sock, and the dog at first goes for the food but soon learns to play with the toy—a sock stuffed with food.

If you want to give your dog toys but don't have the money, try old socks. Other great homemade toys are old denims that you cut in pieces, large and small boxes, empty paper towel rolls, old towels, old shoes, and old slippers. Junk mail can make a great toy, too.

My parents' dog, Mickey, likes to go through the mail. He loves envelopes; the window envelopes are the best because they crinkle. My mom keeps a wastebasket in her office in which she only puts paper and envelopes that Mickey can play with. Nearly every day, when Mom goes into the study to work at her desk, Mickey comes in, sticks his head down into "his" wastebasket and pulls out envelopes. He rips one up, shakes it, then moves on to the next one. Mom says he often falls asleep when he's finished, lying on top of the pile of ripped up paper. Now that's good fun.

My friend Jerri gets toys for her two busy Westie terriers at a thrift store. The store has bags of baby toys (human baby toys) that it sells for a couple bucks per bag. Jerri brings home the bag and throws out anything that could hurt the dogs and then gives them the plastic or plush toys. The dogs are still pretty young, so they end up tearing up a lot of their toys. This is an inexpensive way for Jerri to have an inexhaustible supply of toys to replace the ones she needs to throw out.

You can often find toys out on your walks, too. Dogs love the treasures they find "in the wild." The odd piece of rope, the discarded empty plastic container—as long as you're careful to watch and make sure your dog doesn't eat what she finds, you can let your dog turn some of what she finds into toys.

Mine, Mine, Mine

Muggins knows when a toy is for her. She prances and wags and wiggles. Such importance. Such celebration. New toys make Muggins feel special. I believe she takes comfort in knowing that big pile of toys is available for her.

For a while, I dated a man, Michael, who had a one-year-old yellow Lab, Buck. What Buck put in his mouth, he chewed. That included toys. Therefore, Buck couldn't have squeaky toys, plush toys, or rope toys. He also couldn't have socks because, unlike Muggins, he didn't know the difference between socks that were toys and wearable socks. That left nylabones, tennis balls, and other hard toys. These are the kinds of toys that Muggins has no use for whatsoever.

So when Buck visited, I'd pick up Muggins's basket of toys, everything but the balls and bones. She'd watch me, her tail still, her ears flat against her head. She hated it when I picked up her toys.

After Michael and Buck left, I'd immediately get the basket of toys out again. As soon as the basket was on the floor, Muggins would sniff her possessions, digging around in the pile to pull out her current favorite. I'd leave the room to go do something and the next thing I'd hear is the whuff, whuff, whuff of Muggins trotting across the carpet toward me with a toy in her mouth. She has a special trot when she brings me a toy. It's an eager, hopeful trot, full of energy and expectation.

I'd look up from what I was doing and see her coming toward me with a plush toy or a squeaky toy in her mouth. I'd throw the toy for her. She'd leave and I'd hear her rooting around again in her toy basket. Then I'd hear the whuff, whuff, whuff again, and there she was with another toy.

We'd repeat this process a couple more times until four or more toys were strewn through the house. Then Muggins would lie down in one of her favorite spots, her chin on a plush toy, and she'd go to sleep, content. I swear it seemed like she felt as though she had gotten things back to normal once she'd spread her toys around. All was right in her world again.

Toys provide dogs with fun, obviously. But they do more than that. Dogs need familiarity. Toys give them that. Toys also give dogs a sense of importance, a sense of autonomy— they have something that's theirs. You see it in children, the sense of pride even the smallest toddlers have over their possessions. Dogs have it too.

Your dog loves possessing toys. Dogs like the feeling of knowing what's theirs. You know how dogs get attached to special blankets, dog beds, or towels? These things are theirs, and they know it. They get the same happy feeling of ownership from their toys. So make sure that they have lots of toys nearby, and you'll be making sure your dog is a happy dog.

Home Is Where The Toys Are

When I used to travel with Dizzy, I always took a handful of her toys with me. She'd act a little uncertain when we arrived at our destination. She'd sniff the motel room and stand stiffly in the middle of the room with her tail wagging hesitantly. Then I'd get out her toys.

Her demeanor would change instantly. She'd trot over and root around in the pile, sniffing each toy, then would look up at me and wag her tail. She'd give me a broad doggy smile, then lie down next to her toys. "Okay," she seemed to be saying. "My stuff is here. Everything's all right." Her toys were like a little security blanket, something that helped her find her place in a new situation.

When you travel with your dog, make sure you take along a few of your dog's favorite toys. Keep a couple toys in your car too. When your dog has her own toys, she feels more at home—wherever she is.

To Chew or Not to Chew

Providing dogs with toys is part of being a good dog parent, again, because it makes for a happy, contented dog. But there's also a self-serving reason for giving a dog lots of toys.

One of the most common complaints about dogs is that they chew––furniture, clothes, shoes, you name it. All the dog experts say that a bored dog is a chewing dog. Dogs need to chew—yes. They don't, however, need to chew things that aren't meant to be chewed. Dogs that have lots of their *own* toys to play with don't need to go looking for trouble. They not only have lots of things to stimulate their interest, but they have the satisfaction of possession.

Giving your dog lots of toys keeps her out of trouble. It keeps her busy. It keeps her active. A busy, active dog is one who isn't a headache. When your dog is happily active with her toys, you won't have to worry about her stealing things you don't want her to have. Your dog won't pull things down from tables or chairs or shelves. She won't chew things she isn't supposed to chew. A dog with a lot of toys can be left anywhere, in your home or someone else's, in a motel—it doesn't matter. She won't touch things that aren't hers to touch because you've given her plenty of her own things to play with.

Your dog won't look for toys in the "wrong" places when you provide her with plenty of toys that are her own. Giving dogs lots of possessions makes them well-behaved dogs. A well-behaved dog is a joy to spend time with. So giving your dog lots of toys, providing *her* with fun, brings *you* joy.

It's simple. Giving abundantly leads to receiving abundantly. Nowhere is that more true than in parenting a dog.

chapter 3

Giving Your Dog the Chance to Run Off-Leash

It's impossible to be a good dog parent without exercising your dog. Dogs must have exercise. Actually, everyone must have exercise. Being a couch potato isn't healthy for people or for dogs either. Dogs need exercise to stay healthy. But more important, they need it to be happy. Exercise is fun for dogs.

Daily walks are a good place to start in making sure your dogs get enough exercise. Giving your dog daily walks is essential to being a good dog parent. But if you want to be a great dog parent, you need to go a little further.

Run Wild, Run Free

There's nothing like the joy on a dog's face when the dog is running free, her nose to the wind or the ground, her tail whirring in celebratory circles. This is a dog at her best.

Dogs enjoy being out walking, on or off a leash. They love the fresh air and the cornucopia of smells they encounter, be they city or country smells. But dogs really love being *off* the leash, being free to run and explore.

Muggins doesn't like being on a leash. Most dogs don't.

A friend of mine who used to take care of Muggins when I went out of town told me that Muggins reminded her of an orca whale. When orcas are in captivity, their dorsal fin flops over and lies across their back. When they're out in the ocean, free, their dorsal fin is upright. When Muggins is on a leash, her tail is down and still, dropping over her little tush. When she's off-leash, that tail is upright, the little flag end of white fur waving as it whips around.

Every day, your dogs do what you want them to do. They accommodate you. They stay by your side when you're home. They wait patiently in crates or by the door or in front of the window when you're gone. If you're sitting still, they lie nearby. If you're moving around, they follow you. They live to be with you, to serve you in whatever way they can. It's a small thing, really, for you to offer them some freedom that's just for them.

That's what having a chance to run off-leash does for your dog. Do you remember what it felt like when you were a kid and you got out of school at the end of the day? Do you remember that exhilarating feeling of freedom? I believe that's what dogs feel like when they get off-leash and get to run and explore. They're free. They get time just to be purely dogs.

A Place for Us

Freedom is a powerful euphoric. Giving a dog occasional freedom is one of the best ways to have an emotionally well-adjusted dog. But the freedom needs to be safe freedom. Some people mistakenly think they're doing their dogs a favor by letting them run loose around neighborhoods. Don't do this. Would you let your young kids play in the streets unsupervised? A loose dog is a dog in danger. Find ways to give your dog freedom to run in safe places, away from cars and under close supervision.

I'm lucky enough to live in a rural area with plenty of places for off-leash walks. But even if you live in a city, you can find a place to let your dog run off-leash. When I used to visit a friend in Seattle, we'd take our dogs to off-leash parks—places specifically set up for dogs to run off-leash. Enclosed by a fence and often bounded by a river or a lake, these areas are a doggy heaven. Dogs of every size and variety race unhindered by leashes or chains, playing with new friends, exploring the fauna and jumping headlong into water for an exhilarating swim.

Wherever I've lived, I have always found a place nearby that's safe for a dog to run off-leash. A park, a beach, a forest trail, a college campus—it doesn't matter, as long as the place is away from roads and cars.

Brad and I used to take Dizzy to either a park or the College of William and Mary campus in Virginia. Both were lush, wooded areas safely away from cars where Dizzy could run and explore. She loved it. She'd race ahead of us, checking back over her shoulder now and then to make sure we were still with her. She bolted after squirrels, sniffed around trees, crashed through undergrowth. The whole time her little stub of a tail whipped around in an ecstatic circle.

You'll find you'll get great pleasure when you watch your dog run free. It's almost as though you're experiencing for yourself the same joy that your dog is feeling. If you mostly walk your dog on-leash, she probably enjoys it, but you'll see that she really comes to life when you find a place for her to run free.

Runs Light Up Your Life

Letting your dog run off-leash will keep her full of life and full of enthusiasm. You know how you look forward to vacations and special days? Your life gets a little dull if you don't have those special times to look forward to, doesn't it?

Dogs look forward to off-leash runs. These runs brighten their lives.

Dizzy got arthritis at a young age—six years old. After that, she wasn't so enthusiastic about walking on a leash around the neighborhood. In fact, it got so she would walk to the end of the driveway, sit down and refuse to go any further. I knew she was in pain. A series of visits to the vet confirmed her pain. The diagnosis was severe arthritis, and there was nothing to do for it but give her anti-inflammatories and aspirin. I had to stop taking her with me on my daily walks. It was heartbreaking to leave her behind. She wanted to come, but it just hurt too much.

But when we took Dizzy to the park or on drives up into the mountains, she came to life. Gone was the dog in pain. Out came the puppy with all the enthusiasm and vigor I remembered from her early years. She saved herself, Brad said, for these special walks. We tried to give her as many opportunities as possible to have this freedom, right up until her last months.

If you have an older dog who doesn't get around much anymore, it's easy to give her an off-leash experience. Older dogs, as a general rule, aren't as likely as younger dogs to run off. An older dog's life can get kind of dull, but you can really brighten it by giving her special jaunts in the woods, a meadow or a sandy beach.

Stick with Me

Some dog parents are afraid their dogs will run off if they let them off-leash. And some dogs will. If you want a dog that will stay with you while you walk her off-leash, you need to do two things.

First, make sure you start the off-leash walking in a safe place while your dog is still young. I started running Muggins off-leash when she was only a few months old. This is key to having a dog that will stay nearby even when they're off the leash. If dogs get used to running free while they are still puppies, when they want to be safely near you, they're more likely to stay nearby as adult dogs, too. Teach your dog what's expected early on, and she'll do it for her entire life. It's easier to control a puppy than it is a full-grown dog––at least it's easier to catch a puppy who is running off.

If you get your dog when she is an adult, experiment carefully with off-leash runs. It helps to have more than one person present at the first trial, and it really helps to carry yummy treats in your pockets to lure your dog back if she starts to take off.

Second, make sure you give your dog lots of off-leash walks. Dogs that are rarely off the leash get so worked up about being free that the freedom can go to their heads, and they can run off. If being off-leash is a regular thing, the dog won't be frantic to take advantage of her freedom. Dogs are smart, and they have good memories.

If you walk your dog off-leash at least a couple times a week, your dog will remember the fun, and she'll know that fun will be coming her way again and again. She won't need to run off at the first glimpse of freedom.

Let Me Entertain You

Need a pick-me up? A smile? A good laugh? Take your dog for an off-leash run. I dare you not to feel the joy of your dog's delight.

When a dog is off-leash, she'll often turn into a little entertainer, one who will make you––and everyone who sees her––laugh. Joy is contagious.

When Muggins is off-leash, for example, she loves to carry sticks. Actually, the word "sticks" doesn't describe what she likes to carry. Muggins likes to carry logs or branches and sometimes even small trees. The bigger the limb, the happier she is. She started this when she was a puppy, finding huge sticks four feet or longer to carry. She could barely lift them, but that didn't stop her. She'd find the balance point and pick up the stick. Lifting her head and tail proudly, she'd prance ahead of me with her prize.

As she got older and stronger, she began carrying longer and longer sticks. I've seen her carry, I kid you not, fifteen-foot branches. She's also fond of driftwood logs. After she picks up her treasure, she heads off down the beach, doing a little queenly doggy trot, glancing back over her shoulder to check on me from time to time. This is hilarious to watch. When she looks back, the whole branch carries her in a circle, and she ends up doing a full 360 with the branch in her mouth. Carrying logs and branches is great fun for Muggins, and it's not something she does when she's on a leash.

I've lost count of the number of people I've seen smiling and pointing at Muggins when she carries sticks on our walks. Let your dog spread joy in the world. Let your dog run off-leash, and see what antics she has up her furry sleeves.

Paw to Paw, We Connect

When Muggins was a puppy, we lived just five minutes from a vast park with open fields, a forest, and a small lake with a path around it. The first time we let Muggins off the leash in that park, she took off, bouncing up and down through the tall grass, racing along the paths, circling trees with her nose to the ground. Her stump of a tail, like that of Dizzy before her, whipped in circles. But even as she ran around, she kept turning to check on us and would run back to us at regular intervals.

She loved greeting every dog she saw. She'd dance around them and then take off running, glancing over her shoulder with a coy, come-hither look that clearly said, "Come on, chase me." Most dogs obliged, and the other dog's owner and I would stand around with silly grins on our faces, enjoying the sight of our playing dogs.

That's another bonus for you in letting your dog run off-leash. You'll discover the pleasure of bonding with other like-minded souls. Plus, you'll make new friends.

There's a fellowship that occurs in these situations, whether in parks, on beaches, on trails, or in open fields— anywhere two or more dogs come together to play. Call it "doghood," it's a connection that only true dog parents can really appreciate. You'll rarely learn each other's names; you'll be known as your dog's mom or dad. I am "Muggins's Mom." Dog moms and dads stand together watching their furry babies race in circles, roll around on the ground, wrestle, dodge and weave, and bark and growl in that playful way dogs have when they're pretending to be rough and tough.

Take your dog on off-leash runs and enjoy the new relationships you'll discover in the process. Those relationships will help you be a better dog parent.

While you're standing around watching your dogs, you'll find yourself talking about your dogs. That talk is educational. You'll get a lot of ideas on how to be a great dog parent when you listen to other dog parents talk about how they nurture their furry kids.

Better Than Prozac

Is your dog glum? Does your dog seem lethargic? Before you panic, think for a minute. When was the last time you let your dog run off-leash?

When Muggins is deprived of her off-leash runs for any length of time, she becomes depressed. Her eyes look sad. Her ears droop. Her tail sags. She wanders around the house sighing a lot. She brings me toys and drops them listlessly into my lap, then sits down with a thud, the look on her face clearly communicating that playing with a toy in the house is not the same thing as running loose outside.

Does any of this sound familiar? If your dog is displaying any of these symptoms, a nice off-leash run could be just what the doctor ordered.

A couple years ago, I tried out a new pair of heel liners for my shoes that resulted in a quarter-sized blister on my left heel. The blister was raw, and whenever I tried to put on a shoe, I experienced excruciating pain. After a week, the blister still had not begun to heal, and I finally accepted the reality that I was going to have to rest my foot and allow it to heal before I walked again.

Muggins was glum for two days, but on the third day, she was beyond glum. The bright-eyed, eager, let's-get-to-it look in her eyes was fading, and she moped around. She stood outside the sliding glass door and stared in at me with her best Snoopy-the-vulture impression. I couldn't stand it any more.

Determined to walk, I wore a pair of backless clogs with gaiters over the top. When I got to the beach and let Muggins out of the car, she hit the ground running. She raced off into the tall grass and sprang from clump to clump. Occasionally, I got glimpses of her head, her ears flying. I couldn't walk very fast in the clogs, so I followed slowly. But it was worth it to give Muggins her joy.

If your dog is down and needs her off-leash runs, do what you can to give them to her. If you have to suffer a little discomfort, so be it. If you truly cannot do it physically, see if a trusted friend or family member will help out. You can also hire a professional dog walker (one whose credentials you have thoroughly checked). Pet sitters often will walk a dog for you. See Chapter 19 for guidance on how to find a good pet sitter.

Joy. That's the simple one-word reason for running your dog off-leash. One of your responsibilities as dog parents is to give your dogs joy. Off-leash walks are one of the very best ways to do that.

chapter 4

Walking Your Dog in Any Weather

Okay, here's the deal. Good dog parents take their dogs on daily walks. Great dog parents find places to let their dogs run off-leash. Outstanding dog parents go yet another step and take their dogs out in any and all kinds of weather. Outstanding dog parents rival the U.S. Post Office's mail carriers for tenacity—neither wind nor rain nor sleet shall keep them from their appointed rounds.

Just Do It

One day, I ran into a man I see from time to time on the beach with his dogs. It was bitter cold. We were having an unusual spell of below-freezing weather. We even had snow on the beach, something we rarely see. The rivulets of run-off from the dunes and the access roads had frozen solid across the sand. The wind was biting.

This man has two miniature schnauzers. They were wearing little sweaters, blue for the boy and red for the girl. The man, bundled into a couple of jackets, gloves, and hat, walked briskly into the cold wind. The dogs trotted happily from log to log.

I stopped to talk with the man and commented on the weather we'd had recently—days of pouring rain, one windstorm after the other and freezing cold. "Makes it a little challenging to walk, doesn't it?" I said, conversationally.

He shrugged and smiled. "Yeah. But you have to do it anyway, for them." He motioned to his dogs. "You just do it."

Fleetingly, I wondered if he worked for Nike. But he's right. You have to just do it. Maybe the advertising agency that came up with Nike's slogan employs people who have dogs. Dog walking is the epitome of "Just do it." Giving your dog the freedom to run can't be an optional activity, something you fit in when you have the time or do when it is comfortable or convenient. If you want to be an extraordinary dog parent, you give your dog the freedom to run, and unless you live in one of those states where the weather is balmy year round, you're going to have to endure a little bad weather.

When the Going Gets Tough, the Tough Get Going

With just a few exceptions, I walk nearly every day. I walk for Muggins, who needs her off-leash walks.

In some places, like Florida or California perhaps, the weather aspect of daily walking is probably not that great a challenge. But I live in the Pacific Northwest. I live in one of the wettest places in the world. In the fall, winter, and spring, it often rains six days out of seven. We don't look outside and say, "Oh, look, it's raining today." We look outside and say, "Oh, look, it's sunny today." I actually love rain, but I have to admit that walking on sunny days is easier than walking on the rainy days. Muggins doesn't care either

way. Wet, dry, hot, cold, windy, calm—it's all the same to
Muggins. She just wants to walk.

Well, I take it back. She does have a preference. She
really loves the windy days, those days when the dry sand
is blowing across the wet beach in undulating snakes. Muggins loves chasing those sand snakes. She races after the
blowing sand, barking furiously, her tail wagging in a constant circle.

We often get windstorms here in the winter with gusts
of over 70 miles per hour. When I see my tall fir trees sway-
ing in the wind, when my wind chimes are ringing in a frantic clatter, when it sounds like a long line of freight trains
are roaring through my yard and are about to flatten my
house, I skip walking.

Muggins sulks.

I hate it when Muggins sulks. So I once tried to walk in
gusting wind. I parked the truck and unlatched the door.
The wind whipped the door from my hand and flung it open.
I stepped out of the truck and turned toward the tempest
heaving itself across the beach. Sand raced past me. Muggins took off at full speed. She disappeared into sand clouds
that came up to my hips. I leaned into the wind, muscled the
truck door shut and looked down the beach. Sand got in my
eyes under my contact lens.

I began trudging. I was walking as hard as I could, as
fast as I could. I was barely moving. When I looked down at
the sand whizzing by me at freeway speeds, I felt like I was
going backwards. It made me dizzy. Muggins ran by, her
ears flying, barking madly. I gritted my teeth.

I wanted to get back in my truck and go home. But
Muggins was having such a great time, I didn't have the
heart. I have tried, in the past, sitting in my truck and letting Muggins run around on her own. She won't tolerate it.

She comes back, stands by the driver's door and barks. It's legal to drive on the beach here. Many dog owners drive to the beach, let their dog out of the car and then drive on, letting the dog run behind or beside the car. Even though I think this is a dangerous practice, I tried this method when I hurt my back a few years ago in desperation to get Muggins exercise. Muggins got frantic, racing around in front of the truck to try and stop me. Needless to say, I never tried that again.

So, on that super-windy day, I trudged on. My lungs strained to capture oxygen from the violent air. My calf and thigh muscles ached after only a few steps. I groaned and turned my back to the wind again. I'd gone hardly any distance at all. The safety and warmth of the truck beckoned.

Muggins ran by again, her tail a blur. She barked as she went past, her ears flapping. I sighed and turned back into the wind.

I made it almost a mile down the beach before the gusts increased to such intensity that I could no longer make any forward progress at all. It was all I could do to keep myself upright. Muggins, low to the ground and anchored on four legs, continued her ecstatic pursuit of blowing sand. The sand kicked up even higher than before and got in my eyes again.

"Uncle," I said out loud. It was time to give up. I headed back to the truck. It was like being on roller skates. The wind skimmed me down the beach. I just had to keep my upright balance. Muggins kept merrily chasing sand.

When I finally got back in the truck, I had sand in every nook and cranny of my body—in my hair, in my ears, under my fingernails. I was exhausted, physically and mentally. Muggins jumped into the truck and stared at her treat bag, panting happily.

Was it worth it? Absolutely. To give your dog a gift of pure joy it's worth the fight against gusting wind and raging sand. At least once in awhile.

Being a dog parent sometimes requires what will seem to you like superhuman effort. If you live in a place where the elements don't allow you to walk comfortably every day of the week, you may have to experience some discomfort to make sure your dog has the walks she needs. Yes, it's a bit of a sacrifice, but it's worth it to have a healthy, happy dog.

There's Got to Be an Easier Way

Sometimes, however, you can get creative about how you walk in tough weather. For instance, now that I'm married to Tim, I have a better way of walking in gusting wind. Tim drops off Muggins and me at one point on the beach. Muggins and I walk with the wind behind us for an hour. I use my cell phone to call Tim, and he comes to get us. I still get buffeted about and drenched, but at least I don't have to work as hard.

This is a great way to deal with wind. As for rain and snow, you may need a little mechanical help, like a golf cart or maybe a snowmobile. Handling most elements, however, can be done with only a little special outdoor gear.

Don't You Wish You Had a Fur Coat?

With proper outdoor gear, you can give your dog a gift of freedom that isn't hinged on the weather. A good dog parent learns to be creative. You can find rain gear, snowsuits, the right footwear, whatever it takes. If it's too hot, you can walk early. Stay in the shade, carry plenty of water, and wear wide-brimmed hats and loose, breathable clothing. If it's too cold, you can get insulated clothing for you and your dog. By properly attiring yourself and your dog, you can walk in most weather.

On stormy days, I wear a full Gortex rain suit, the hood up and tied tightly around my face, a neoprene facemask with a polar fleece neck wrap, a polar fleece headband, and water resistant shoes and gloves. You can find these in any outdoor catalog or store. The initial investment is a bit pricey, but giving your dog these walks improves her health, and what you spend on special gear can save you money on vet bills later.

Your dog can wear special clothes too. My friend with the schnauzers has little raincoats for his dogs. Dizzy used to wear one when she walked. Dogs with thick coats meant for the outdoors, like Muggins, for instance, don't need special coats. But if your dog doesn't have such a coat, invest in a sweater or raincoat for your dog.

If you're walking your dog in the snow, try those little dog booties you can get in any pet store or catalog. Most dogs will learn to wear them. If you walk in the sun, you can get your dog sunglasses.

For the Joy of It

You may grouse about the weather and pray silently for a few calm, dry days to give you easy walking time, but don't let much stop you from walking. Weather is an outside force over which you have no control. Don't allow it to dictate when and how much joy you give your dog. You're in control of how much joy you can provide for your dog, how many ecstatic experiences of freedom you can squeeze into her all-too-short life. Sometimes forces are greater than your ability to give her the chance to run. You can't do battle with truly inclement weather. But you can overcome the inconveniences of a little bad weather. You can, because you're an outstanding dog parent.

The benefits and blessings you'll get from walks with your dog will permeate your entire life. Add a treat to your day. Breathe in fresh air, and soak in your dog's joy. Your dog's delighted prance is a celebration of life that's inspiring.

chapter 5

Letting Your Dog Get Dirty

Have you ever noticed that children whose parents are obsessed with keeping them and their clothes clean don't have as much fun as other kids? Having to worry about keeping clean limits kids, and kids need to be able to play with abandon, even if it means getting totally filthy. The same goes for dogs. Dogs who aren't allowed to get dirty because the dirt might get in the house or car do not have as much fun as other dogs. Good dog parents know this. You aren't bothered by a little dirt. You must be more concerned with making sure your dogs have fun.

What's Wrong with a Little Dirt?

Being a dog parent requires some sacrifice. I'm sure you've figured that out by now. One of the sacrifices you need to make is giving up on having perfectly clean surroundings. With a dog in your life, perfect cleanliness just isn't possible—not if you want a happy dog.

I love my parents. They're wonderful people and wonderful parents. They're always there for me when I need them, and they're great grandparents to my dog.

Do you hear a "but" coming? Here it is. My parents are sticklers for "clean." I don't mean just a little clean. I mean really, really clean. I admire this about my parents. In fact, I'm in awe of it. And I'm not the only one in awe. When they last sold a home, an inspector poking around the baseboards and window casings was amazed at the complete and total lack of dirt, and he asked, "Does anyone really live here?" He said he had never in all his years of inspecting homes seen such a clean house.

My parents have a dog, a blonde cocker spaniel named Mickey. Before Mickey, they had a blonde cocker named Corki. Before Corki, they had Shorty, the dog I grew up with. My parents love dogs, and except for a few years here and there, they've always had one.

But dogs are a problem for my parents. Because dogs get dirty.

This bothers my parents. When I visit, Muggins, who loves to run around outside and explore the flower beds, always brings in pieces of bark, grass, or leaves and deposits them in strategic places on the floor and the furniture in my parents' home. Between these little canine flora offerings and the copious amounts of white hair Muggins leaves behind, my mother always has to get out the vacuum when we leave. So she tells me. Feeling a little guilty for forcing her to clean every time I visit, I once sarcastically suggested that we simply attach a Dustbuster to Muggins's tail and be done with the problem. Mom countered with a better idea. Why don't we, she asked, just laminate Muggins? That way, she won't shed or pick up bits of the outdoors in her fur.

Now, why didn't I think of that?

Of course, unless you have one of those rare dog breeds that doesn't shed, or you have enough money to have a housekeeping staff that constantly vacuums wherever your dog goes, you're going to have dog hair in your house. If your dog goes outside, you're going to have dirt, leaves, twigs, and grass in your house.

This is okay. Truly. A little dirt isn't going to hurt you. When you relax your standards just a bit—I'm not suggesting your turn into a slob—you'll enjoy your dog, and your life, a lot more.

Muggins sheds all over my house every day, and every time she comes in from the yard, she brings some delightful bit of it with her. She also brings a little bit of the beach home with her every time we walk, which is almost every day. And I do not, I assure you, vacuum every day. I have better things to do. So my house isn't perfectly clean. If your dog is having a lot of happy fun, and if you have a normally busy life, yours won't be either. To be a good dog parent, you need to learn to live with imperfection.

Too Much Clean Means Not Enough Fun

Like I said, I admire an interest in keeping things clean. It's great if you're willing to vacuum often and clean out the inside of your vehicle every time you take your dog to the woods or the beach. I love being in a clean house and clean car, so I can understand the motivation to clean this much. It's not that I dislike clean. I like it. I just don't like doing it all the time.

Even if you're willing to clean all the time, there is one thing about a penchant for cleanliness that can keep you from being a good dog parent. Being *too* clean can limit your dog's life.

You may allow your dog to be a dog most of the time. You let your dog play and run around in her yard. You take her for walks. You snuggle with her. You let your dog sleep on the furniture and in your bed. You give her plenty of treats. You take her for rides in the car when you go places. You have a very lucky dog.

But do you sometimes not allow your dog to do things because, if she did, she'd get dirty?

I know some people who won't take their dog for a walk if it has recently rained. Mind you, the day is now clear and dry, but it's just that the roads are still wet. These people won't walk their dog because the dog's belly will get dirty. I know other people who won't let their dog play in the yard on wet days. They won't let their dog out to poke around because it's wet and she'll track in dirt.

I understand the reasoning here, and I certainly respect it. But these people have chosen to have clean surroundings over giving their dog more freedom.

I've made a different choice. Muggins runs my household. (This should be obvious by now.) And she loves her yard. She also loves the beach. She loves the rain, and she loves puddles, the muddier the better. I will not curtail her enjoyment of these loves because of a little dirt.

If you want to be a good dog parent, you need to be a little more like me. Yes, your carpet may be a little soiled along a path from the door to the kitchen. Yes, your furniture may be dingier than it could be. Yes, your vehicle may be full of dog hair or sand. And yes, you may have sand and leaves in your bed from time to time. Yes, you have to clean more often than you would prefer. But if you want to be a great dog parent, you can live with all this. If it means you have a happy dog, of course you can live with it.

My mother told me one day that she'd been talking to a man in the grocery store parking lot who had a black-and-white springer spaniel in the car with him. She told him that her granddog was a black-and-white springer, and that her granddog loved the beach. She asked the man if he took his dog to the beach. He said he'd taken the dog there a few times, but she got so dirty that he stopped.

That made even my mother sad. She loves clean. But she also knows how important beach fun is to dogs. Whenever she's taken care of Muggins for any length of time, she has always managed to get in Muggins's walks. She may be vacuuming herself to death, but she lets Muggins have her fun.

How sad for the springer who isn't allowed to play on a beach that's only minutes away because her people are concerned about a little dirt. And how sad for the people who own the dog! I can't even begin to describe the hours and hours of joy and laughter I've had on the beach watching Muggins playing with other dogs, chasing the blowing sand or a flock of sandpipers, or romping through the surf.

Scrub-a-Dub-Dub

Yeah, your dog will get dirty. Accept it. Then set up some easy ways to make for quick and easy canine cleanup.

You see, if you're creative, you can come up with ways to adapt to a dog's capacity to bring dirt into your life. As you'll read in Chapter 12, you can purchase specific styles of carpet and furniture that are designed not to show too much dirt. You can invest in a good vacuum cleaner and a carpet cleaner. You can cover things that you really need to protect.

For example, in order to keep too much of the backyard from getting into our bed, because Muggins sleeps with me and Tim (as described in Chapter 17), I put a sheet on top of the blanket in the bed. It protects the bedding and keeps most of Muggins's dirty offerings away from where we actually lie down. If some gets under the sheets, I have a little whisk broom next to the bed I use to sweep it out. And of course, there's always that handy thing called a washing machine.

I also had a bathtub installed on a platform in my garage so I can easily rinse the dirt off Muggins after her romps. You may not be able to do this, but you could have a sprayer attachment installed near your bathtub. Or you could teach your dog to shower with you.

You can keep a few mini vacuums or carpet sweepers in several areas of your house. You can get a carpet shampooer and make it a habit to shampoo your carpets every couple months. Sound like a lot of work? It's not so bad. Maybe it takes a little more work to keep your surroundings clean if you let your dog get dirty. But it won't kill you to vacuum a little more. As my mom points out, vacuuming burns calories and gets your heart rate up. Cleaning is good for you.

So is having a dirty dog. Well, a *constantly* dirty dog may not be good. But a dog that's allowed to get dirty is a dog that's allowed to be a dog, and a dog that's allowed to be a dog is a dog that's being allowed as much fun as possible. As a dog parent, it's your responsibility to give your dogs that fun. A little dirt is a small price to pay.

chapter 6

Making Sure Your Dog Has a View

Everyone knows babies and small children need stimulation. That's why cribs have mobiles hanging over them, and that's why you involve your children in a variety of activities at an early age. A stimulated mind is a creative mind. A creative mind is generally a well-adjusted mind. Good parents wouldn't dream of locking a child into a room without access to the outside world. It would kill the child's spirit.

Life Can Be Such a Yawn

Dog owners who keep dogs around for fun and companionship sometimes forget that their dogs have a soul, a spirit that can be nurtured or killed. As a good dog parent, you must be interested in keeping your dog's spirit alive. Toys, walks, rides in the car, cuddling, and all the other activities I write about in this book will help you keep the canine spirit alive and well. But no matter how much you love your dogs, and no matter how great a dog parent you are, there will be times when you can't interact with your dog. You do have to leave your dog alone at times. You do have to let your dog entertain herself while you attend to life's necessities like work or housecleaning.

Sometimes, if you're lucky, your dog can come along for the ride, so to speak. My friend's basset hound, Casey, loved to play with "Mr. Vacuum." My friend's housecleaning time was Casey's favorite playtime. Another friend was able to take her dog to work with her, and the dog "helped" her by greeting her retail customers. Not all of us are fortunate enough, however, to engage in activities that always include our dogs. The result is that your dog will spend a lot of time just hanging out with nothing much to do. Dogs sleep a lot, and that's fine. But good dog parents don't want their dogs to sleep their lives away.

A Room with a View

When Muggins is just hanging out, say while I'm busy at my computer or otherwise occupied in the house in a way that she can't be actively included, she spends a lot of time staring out the window. I live on a pretty quiet street in a small town. Not many cars go by. Even so, there are things to watch. Birds are a constant visitor to my yard. Muggins can watch everything from the tiny flitting hummingbirds to the fat, orange-breasted robins. Sometimes squirrels or chipmunks visit. Out the front window, Muggins occasionally spots deer, rabbits, or the neighbors' cats. She keeps an eye on the occasional passing cars and people. The people walking dogs, of course, are the most interesting. Bicycles are fascinating too. She also watches for delivery people or other visitors. The things that go on outside her window provide her with hours of entertainment.

Years ago, I knew a couple who had a standard poodle named Henry. Henry was a great dog, a down-to-earth fellow who was laid back, patient, and easy to please. His idea of a great time was lying on the sofa near the big picture window at the front of my friends' home. They lived in a city, and their street bustled with activity. Henry was fascinated by it all. My friends called their picture window "Poodle TV."

Dizzy used to lie in front of the sliding glass door in every place we lived. She loved to stare out at her backyard and make sure all was quiet on the back forty. Muggins took over Dizzy's spot after Dizzy died. The sliding glass doors in my homes have always been covered with doggy nose prints.

When I had my current home built, I wanted Muggins to be able to see outside from any room in the house. As I explain dogs want to be as close to you as possible. If the window that allows your dog to see outside is on one end of the house and you're on the other, you will have a conflicted canine.

This is why you want to provide your dog as many viewing locations as possible. You don't want to force your dog to choose between entertainment and loyalty. You need to provide "canine TV" in as many rooms as possible.

Interior Design, Canine Style

Muggins can see out every window in our house, as every outrageously happy canine should be able to. The bed in our bedroom is positioned so she can lie on the foot of it and watch the backyard. I've placed a loveseat in front of the window in my office so she can watch the birds hopping around on the branches just outside the window. The living room has the sliding glass door looking out onto the deck and into the woods of the backyard. Two front windows look out to the street. I spent an extra $100 per window when I had the house built to have tempered glass put in so the windows could be placed just ten inches off the floor, perfect chin-resting level for a reclining dog. Muggins can lie in her dog bed in one room to see outside, and the other room has a sofa that she likes to sprawl over the back of to keep an eye on the front yard and the street.

I realize that not everyone can design their house to allow for window accessibility for their dogs. However, even if the windows aren't in the right place, you can help your dog use them by strategically placing your furniture.

Choose the window or windows that provide the most interesting views. From a canine's perspective, an interesting view is one with activity. You want to give your dog access to a window that looks out over the road or out into a natural area where birds or other critters play.

If the window is close enough to the floor for your dog to look out, your job is easy. Just place a dog bed on the floor in front of the window. If the window is higher up, however, you may need to move your furniture around. Place a piece of plush furniture, such as a sofa or chair, under the window. Or position your bed so your dog can lie on the bed to look outside. If these arrangements aren't possible, perhaps you can place a chest under the window and put a cushion on top or just pile up a couple of cushions. You can get old chair cushions or floor pillows cheap at secondhand stores. The goal is to provide a soft perch for your dog so she can look outside. Dogs want to be able to lie down and get comfy when they're entertained. Who can blame them? Do you like watching television standing up?

Does all of this take a little time? Yes. Does it cost money? It could. Is it worth it? Absolutely.

Walk around your home. Do you have enough places for your dog to perch and comfortably keep an eye on what's going on outside? If not, start making changes. Your dog will be a lot happier if you do.

You expect your dog to spend a lot of time just waiting around. In return, as a good dog parent, you need to provide as much entertainment for your dog as possible. A well-positioned window to the outside world is an important part of a dog's enjoyment of the day.

They say the eyes are the window to the soul. This may be; I don't know. I do know that the windows in your homes give a canine's soul access to stimulation, which is essential to fun. Even in the quiet moments, your dogs can have their fun. Make sure your dog can watch the world go by. You get to go to concerts, plays, and sporting events. It's only fair that you provide a little canine theatre for your dogs.

chapter 7

Making Car Travel Fun
for Your Dog

Most dogs love to ride in the car. The image of a dog riding in a car with her head out the window is ubiquitous. Most dogs know the word "car" and some variation of the question, "Do you want to go in the car?"

Most dog parents love to have their dogs along with them in the car. But great dog parents want more than just to have their dogs lie quietly in the car. You want car trips to be fun for your dog.

One of my favorite television commercials is the Nissan ad in which the dog steers his master's recliner to the closest Nissan dealer, bringing the chair to a stop in front of a showroom containing a pick-up. The punch line—"Dogs love trucks." So true.

Beyond Sticking Your Snout
out the Window

Even though dogs love just riding in the car, it can be a somewhat boring time for them, especially if you're traveling too fast for it to be safe to stick their heads out the window. After the initial excitement of getting in the car and getting on the road is over, all there is for a dog to do is stare out the window or lie down and sleep until you reach your destination. You can make your dog's life much more fun if you make car travel interactive.

Muggins has always been intrigued by other dogs and even more so by cats. She knows the words "doggy" and "kitty-cat." She learned those words when she was a puppy.

When she was a pup, as we drove down the road, if she saw a dog or a cat, she'd hop up and down in the back of the truck and bark or whine. I could have discouraged this behavior. Some of my friends and family wish I *had* discouraged this behavior.

But I didn't. I knew Muggins enjoyed having me acknowledge what she'd spotted. All I had to do was say, "Is that a doggy?" or "Is that a kitty-cat?" or even just "Oh, doggy." It was important to say it in the right tone of voice, very excited as if she was spotting something unique and even a little amazing. When I did this, Muggins's eyes lit up, her face brightened, and she held herself a bit straighter. *I spotted a doggy,* she was telling me. She was so proud.

I'd give her a treat. Thus encouraged, she'd return to looking for doggies and kitties. Then we moved on to horsies and cows. Muggins knows the words "doggy," "kitty-cat," "horsie," "deer," "sheep," "bunny," "squirrel," "goose," "duck," and "birdie."

If you want your dog to have this kind of fun, all you need to do is give her a little encouragement. When you pass a dog, cat, horse, or deer, point to the animal and say its name in an animated voice. Then address your dog. "Do you see the doggie?" (It's not essential that you add the "ie" as I have done. I just think it's fun. Try it. You might like it too.)

Your dog will pick up on your enthusiasm and will probably look with interest at what you're indicating. If she shows any excitement, reward with a treat. Pretty soon, your dog will be scanning the sides of the road for animals. You'll have a happy dog with a wagging tail who loves to ride in the car because she gets to spot critters.

Encouraging your dog to bark at cows and horses and the like may result in a great deal of noise, and it may cost you an arm and a leg in kibble for treats. But it enhances your dog's life. It makes your dog feel important. It jazzes up the trips you take. As a good dog parent, you should observe your dog's responses and try to make interesting sights a part of your route as often as possible.

Banishment Isn't for Happy Canines

Michael, my old date who owns Buck, the yellow Lab, had one of those dog barriers in the back of his station wagon. He kept Buck crated in the back of the car while he drove. When Muggins and I were in the car, she had to be crated there too. She hated it. I hated it. I knew it was safer for her than letting her roam in a vehicle the way I do. But I'd look over my shoulder constantly and cringe when I saw her sweet face peering out between the bars, her ears down at the side of her head, her tail still.

When you're with your dog, you need to be *with* your dog. Dogs get frustrated when they're nearby but not near.

Michael obviously was a dog owner, not a dog parent. Along with many others like him, he thought that dogs, like kids, according to the old adage, should be seen and not heard. He could put his dog in the back of his car and that was that. Dog parents don't do this. You don't just cart your dog around in the car. You travel with her. You connect with her.

It's fun being able to talk to your dog and get a response. If you make your car travel interactive, you might find yourself scanning open fields for cows and horses. You might find yourself looking for dogs and cats and deer. Have fun rewarding your dog for spotting one of these critters. Your dog's having fun, and when she's having fun, you'll have fun too. Your dog's excitement can be rewarding for you too.

Being in the car with your dog when you teach your dog to interact with you this way is like traveling with a person. Your dog won't just take up space and get hair and dirt all over the car (although she'll do those things, too). Your dog will comfort you with the knowledge that you have someone to interact with as you're driving down the road. And as I said, it's fun for your dog, and part of your responsibility as a dog parent is to provide her with as much fun as you can.

Look, up ahead, is it a bird, a plane? Or maybe a horsie. That's worth a bark and bounce. And definitely a smile.

chapter 8

Celebrating Your Dog's Birthday and Other Holidays

Holidays are important times in our lives. They're a ritual of celebration and love that we share with the people who mean the most to us.

Even dog owners want to include their dogs in these celebrations. According to an article in *USA Weekend,* about 70 percent of pet owners celebrate their animal's birthdays. This is only right. Dogs are love. That's their purpose here on this earth, to love you and be loved by you. Dogs are the best teachers of unconditional love in the world. How awful it is, then, if you don't include them during those special times when you celebrate love and life. Dogs understand much more than we often give them credit for. They understand celebration. Celebration is fun for dogs.

Happy Birthday to You

I've always celebrated my dogs' birthdays, even when I was just a dog owner. Shorty, my childhood canine companion, got a new toy and a Hostess cupcake for her birthday. (I've learned since then that sugar and chocolate aren't good for dogs.) Dizzy received similar treats.

On Dizzy's fifth birthday, Brad and I had to host a party for the new summer interns at his law firm. Because it landed on Dizzy's birthday, we made it a birthday party, complete with a decorated cake that said, "Happy Birthday Dizzy." I know that many of our guests thought it was a joke and many of those who knew it wasn't a joke thought it was silly. I didn't care. This was the day Dizzy's life began, and it was a day to be celebrated. She had a wonderful time as the center of attention. I believe she may have known we were celebrating her birthday.

I've learned a bit about the downsides of feeding dogs sweets and junk food since Dizzy, so Muggins gets a chicken and cottage cheese "cake" on her birthday. She loves it. Here's how to make a canine-healthy cake:

1. Form two parts ground meat (chicken, turkey, or beef are fine) and one part cottage cheese into a thick patty.

2. Cook over low heat in a nonstick skillet sprayed with cooking spray. Turn the patty after a few minutes so you can cook it evenly on both sides. The cooking time will vary depending on the size of the cake.

3. Poke a fork gently into the middle of the patty to check for doneness. When the juices run clear, the cake is done.

4. Remove it from the pan and set it on a plate to cool. Make sure the cake is cool enough to be eaten before you serve it to your dog. Your dog doesn't know to blow on something when it's too hot, and you don't want the birthday dog to get a scalded tongue.

Once the cake is cool, you can stick birthday candles in it. Use a mechanical lighter to light the candles because you want to get them all burning as fast as possible so they don't drip on the cake. Melted wax isn't good for your dog. If your dog isn't timid about candles as Muggins is, you may need to keep the cake on the counter until you blow out the candles and remove them. It's fun getting that picture of your dog with her cake, but the picture isn't worth burning fur. If your dog goes for the cake even with the candles lit, settle for a picture of your dog scarfing down her special treat.

Be sure you get your dog a new toy for her birthday. You can wrap a dog's present easily. Dogs don't care much about wrapping. So a brown paper shopping bag will do. Fold over the top and tape it.

When you give the gift to your dog, rattle the package. If the toy has a squeaker or other sound-emitting device, squeeze the toy so your dog knows a toy is inside the bag. With proper encouragement, most dogs will rip the bag open with their teeth. If your dog doesn't understand this, get down on the floor and rip the bag open a little at a time. Encourage your dog to stick her nose in and sniff the toy. This often will get her to continue the package opening on her own. If not, keep helping until the toy is revealed.

A Holly, Jolly Canine Christmas

You'll want to include your dog in your celebration of the holidays (Christmas or Hanukah or whatever holiday you acknowledge) as well. When you hang the stockings, for example, hang a small stocking for your dog too. On Christmas morning, put a toy or treats in the stocking.

When my husband and I do this for Muggins on Christmas morning, her nose finds the toy right away. She takes up a standing vigil on the floor beneath her stocking, staring up at it with longing. She usually serenades me with her version of Christmas carols at that point as well—"Arrwoo, yip, roooof, arwoo!" I think this might be "Jingle Bells." I know it isn't "Silent Night."

Most dogs love the excitement of present opening and other celebrations. Invite them to join you. Encourage them to play with the paper. Encourage them to join in singing and dancing and laughter. Dogs love to party. Don't leave yours out of the fun.

Any Excuse to Party

When you include your dog in holidays, don't stop with birthdays and Christmas. You can include your dog in pretty much any holiday. When you ring in the New Year, be sure your dog gets a kiss and a hug at midnight if you're home. If you're not home, be sure to give her that kiss as soon as you walk in the door.

Get your dog a plush groundhog toy (or something that looks like a groundhog) on Groundhog Day.

Give your dog a new red toy on Valentine's Day, and be sure you shower her with love that day. Dress her up in a red collar or bandana.

Your dog can wear green on St. Patrick's Day. And you can put some potato, which most dogs love and which is a good Irish food, in your dog's dinner that day.

Every dog deserves an Easter basket filled with special treats and a new toy. Do not put chocolate in the basket.

You might also choose to give your dog a hard-boiled egg. Most dogs love eggs.

Of course, you'll want to include your dog in Mother's Day. Muggins always gives me a gift and card on Mother's Day. (My husband, Tim, helps out with this. When I was single, my parents helped.) The same goes with Father's Day.

On July Fourth, be sure you include your dog in the picnics and barbecues. You can find a lot of cute red-white-and-blue canine fashions—at the very least, tie a red, white, or blue bandana around your dog's neck. Be sure not to give your dog too much rich food. And be sure you keep your dog away from fireworks of any kind. Fireworks can kill.

On Halloween, give your dog a special treat. If you want, you can dress your dog in costume. Just be sure it's not a costume that will annoy or endanger your dog. Dogs aren't big fans of things pressing their ears down against the sides of their heads, and you don't want anything that curtails your dog's ability to move any way she wants to move. Be sure you keep your dog away from candy. Dogs have been known to eat candy with the wrapper on—both candy and wrappers are quite unhealthy. You can usually find Halloween-themed toys in pet catalogs. Buy your dog a plush ghost or black cat.

Thanksgiving is a great holiday for dogs because most dogs love turkey. If your dog isn't allergic, it's fine to give her a little white meat on that special day. Not too much— again, too much rich food can make your dog sick. Be sure you give thanks for your dog on Thanksgiving. Can there be a greater blessing than a loyal dog that loves you no matter what you say or do?

Don't forget to include your dog in your birthdays and in anniversaries as well. You might let your dog have a little tidbit of meat from your special meal. If you take a romantic trip, consider bringing your dog along.

Here's one caveat concerning the festivities. If you're celebrating a holiday and you have more than one dog, or you celebrate a holiday with someone else who also has a dog, it's a good idea to get the same toy for every dog when you buy the dogs gifts. Dogs aren't really big on sharing.

Ritual's Good for the Spirit

Ritual is very important to dogs. Routine. Structure. They like to know what's going to happen, what's expected of them. But they also like celebration because it's exciting and different.

So what could be better than a holiday ritual? It's familiar—after only a couple of holidays, dogs catch on to what's going to happen, what they can expect. They know what it means to open a present and get a new toy. They know what it means to eat a special cake or get special treats in their stocking. They know what it means to have someone fussing over them. It's a special kind of fun.

As much as it's familiar, it's also different. Dogs know this. Your dog will know that these days don't come often. They'll pick up on your excitement and share your celebratory mood. Anything you can do to involve your dog in the festivities will make holidays more fun for your dog.

But it's not just for them. You get plenty from celebrating with your dog, too. What could be more enriching than pulling another being into the fold of love and celebration in your lives? Have you ever invited a friend who can't go home for Christmas to share the holiday with you? Have you ever taken a casual friend a birthday gift and seen his face light up in surprise and delight, heard him tell you how much it means to him?

Dogs are no different. You're bringing light and love into your dog's life. You're not only validating her importance in your world, you're celebrating her very existence. Even if she doesn't understand the concept of a birthday, she knows when she's the center of attention.

It's an opportunity to make your dog feel special, and the bonus is that you also get to feel the joy of gifting another being with love. It's as good as having a birthday yourself.

PART II: COMFORT

Dogs are an amazing source of comfort. They keep you company when you're down. They can keep you warm. They can even lower your blood pressure. Of course, you want to give your dog as much comfort as she gives you.

Dogs are adaptable creatures. They learn to adjust to whatever conditions in which they find themselves, but good dog parents don't want their dog to have to adjust. You want to provide your dog with as much comfort as your dog provides you.

Good dog parents feed their dog a healthy diet. You're willing to get your dog the best care, whatever that takes. You give your dog massages. You buy furniture with your dog's comfort in mind. You have plenty of comfortable places in the house for the dog to sleep. If your dog steals your spot on the sofa when you get up, you let the dog stay there. You groom and dress your dog well when necessary. You always have treats handy. You let your dog sleep with you.

A dog will lie in the dirt in pouring rain to be near you. But she will be much happier if she can lie on a cushion. A good dog parent knows this. You give your dog the comfortable life all dogs deserve.

chapter 9

Feeding Your Dog
a Healthy Diet

Dogs love people food. If you give your dog half a chance, she will happily eat pretty much anything you eat. This is fine if you eat healthy foods that are good for dogs. Many dogs, for example, love fruits and vegetables, and several of these are good for dogs (and you too). Most dogs, though, also like junk food too, and that's not good.

Tastes Great—Why Not Eat It?

A dog will eat anything that tastes good to her, whether or not it will hurt her.

Good dog parents do better for their dogs than they do for themselves. You may not be able to resist chocolate cheesecake, but you sure know better than to feed it to your dog. You want a healthy dog, right? So you need to do whatever it takes to have a healthy dog, even if it means "depriving" your canine baby of the goodies she whines for.

Dogs just don't know what's good for them, or more specifically what's not good for them.

Many dogs love chocolate. Mine drools like crazy when anyone is eating it. But chocolate is potentially fatal to dogs. Anything that is junk food for you is also junk food for your dog. You may not be able to resist foods that are bad for you (I know I often can't), but don't feed them to your dog. Also keep an eye on your dog on your walks. Dogs will eat pretty much anything they find, and some of those finds—like fish carcasses or spoiled food—can be terribly dangerous to dogs.

The Voice of Nutritional Reason

Muggins developed an inflammatory bowel disease when she was only a few months old. Table food, the vet told me, was a big no-no for Muggins. She could have carrots, turkey, and chicken. But that was it. The vet told me to feed her only a specific kind of dog food. I'd put the dry food in a plastic cup and feed it to her bite by bite while we ate. It made her feel like she was taking part in our meal, and she never seemed to mind that she wasn't getting the real deal.

She eventually appeared to grow out of the illness, and for a while she was able to eat more variety. Even so, I've always kept her bites of people food to a bare minimum, and I've always been careful not to feed her junk. It's bad enough that I ate the junk I ate; I didn't need to feed it to Muggins.

On the flip side, I've decided that what's healthy and right for me may not be the best for Muggins. I'm a vegetarian. I've looked into vegetarian treats and dog food. But after reading about a dog's nutritional needs, I've concluded that dogs need meat. I could be wrong. Maybe my next dog will be a vegetarian, but for now, Muggins gets meat.

Your job as a dog parent is not to feed your dog what you like or what is convenient for you to buy. Your job is to determine what's best for your dog. To do this, speak to your vet. Better yet, find a vet that specializes in canine nutrition. Or buy a book on the subject. There's an enormous amount

of information out there about canine nutrition. Just
human nutrition, not all the information is consister
need to be willing to experiment and change directions if
what you're doing isn't working for your dog.

Gotta Love a Home-Cooked Meal

Muggins is now fed mostly a home-cooked diet. Her inflammatory bowel disease flared up again three years ago, and I've had
to be very careful about what she eats. Dr. Patti Schaefer recommended a tremendous resource that has guided me in preparing Muggins's meals—*Home-Prepared Dog & Cat Diets*—*The
Healthful Alternative*, by Donald R. Strombeck, D.V.M., Ph.D.
Combining the advice I have gotten in this book with the prescription dog foods that my veterinarians have recommended, I
have found a combination of food that seems to suit Muggins.

It's hard to know what's best to feed your dog. According to *Home-Prepared Dog & Cat Diets,* a home-prepared
diet consisting of whole foods is ideal for your dogs. If it's at
all possible, I highly recommend home-cooking your dog's
food. Everyone I've spoken to and everything I've read indicates that dogs fare better when you feed them real, whole,
healthy food, either raw or cooked.

When you home-cook your dog's food, you can prepare a few days worth at a time and put the food in plastic
containers or bags. You can bring this prepared food along
with you when you're on the road with your dog.

I understand, however, that this isn't practical for a lot of
busy people. Preparing the meals we feed to Muggins is rather
time-consuming. It's worth it because it has made a huge difference in her health, but not everyone can do this. What can
you do if you don't have the time to cook for your dog?

If It Has to Be Fast Food, Make It the Best

If you're going to feed your dog a prepared diet, you need to do some research to find the best food. The *Whole Dog Journal* suggests that you look for several things when choosing a food. It should be processed at low heat; have high bioavailability (such as chelated vitamins and minerals); have high-quality ingredients such as meats, grains, and vegetables; have no artificial additives; have natural preservatives; have no refined sugars; and be meat or protein based.

These are tough standards. The *Whole Dog Journal*, which you can find online at *www.whole-dog-journal.com*, has a great, thorough report on the best natural dog foods around. It's a good place to get the information you need to make the best choice for your dog.

Caroline Knapp, author of *Pack of Two*, discovered when she got her puppy, Lucille, that everyone had an opinion on what to feed a dog. "What are you feeding her?" Knapp was asked by other dog owners. These same owners gave her their opinions. She was told, "Iams is best: lamb and rice. No, Eukanuba's best. No, Hill's Science Diet."

You're going to get a lot of competing information about diet. Some of the process just involves a little trial and error. Pick a food that seems to be healthy, and see how your dog does on it. Monitor your dog's health. If your dog is doing well, you can stick with the diet you've chosen.

Do I Have to Take My Vitamins?

In addition to food, it's important to find the right supplements for your dog. This also requires research, and every dog's needs are different. For years, I have fed Muggins algae, a natural source of the chelated vitamins and minerals that The Whole Dog Journal says your dogs need. I've found that her recurring severe ear infections have cleared up entirely since she started on it. She also gets a multivitamin and an array of herbs and other supplements to help with her bowel condition. She also gets enzymes. Enzymes help your dog digest her food, and that makes her healthier overall.

To find out what food and supplements your dog may need, do some research online. Check out books on dog nutrition, and talk to a vet who has a holistic approach to practicing medicine. A good dog parent doesn't just dump the cheapest dog food in a bowl and call it good. You must find the best food and the best supplements to give your dog the best health possible. If your dog has any physical ailments, like Muggins and her bowel disease, you need to monitor her diet even more carefully.

Forget Drinking from the Toilet

Dogs need water too. Be sure you provide your dog with plenty of fresh, healthy water. I filter my water, and I give the same water to Muggins. Why would I give her what I won't drink myself?

If you have good water in your town, tap water is fine for your dog. But if your water is the least bit questionable, filter it or buy bottled water for your dog.

Little details like these can really improve the quality of your dog's life. We all know that healthy dogs tend to live longer too. Need I say more?

chapter 10

Getting the Best Care for Your Dog

Some people pick veterinarians the same way they choose grocery stores. They go to the closest one or to the one that has the best prices. That's it. They have little concern for quality of care. They have no interest in the vet's background or track record.

These people are dog owners. Dog *parents,* on the other hand, know they must get the best care possible for their dogs.

What's Up, Doc?

I live in a small town. When I first moved here, the town did have a vet, and it would have been very convenient for me to take my dog there because the office was minutes from my home. However, I never took her to that vet because the things I'd heard from other dog parents and owners were not so good. For six years, I drove nearly an hour to a vet in a town forty-five miles from my house. Of course, there were other vets closer to where I live, but I chose the vet who I thought would give the best care. I was willing to drive to get that care.

I spoke to people who had healthy animals that they loved in the same way I love my dog, and I asked them where they'd recommend taking my dog for veterinary care. When I got a ringing endorsement, I made an appointment and checked out the vet myself.

Even if you're new in a town, as I was, you can always find someone to talk to about vet care. It's easy. Just stop and talk to anyone walking a dog. If you're out walking your dog regularly, as a good dog parent must, you'll see a lot of people with their dogs. Ask where they take their dogs to the vet. Then ask why. If they tell you it's because it's close by, take their recommendation with a grain of salt. Talk to as many people with dogs as you can.

Dog parents love to talk to other dog parents. You can tell immediately whether someone is a dog parent or a dog owner. You can tell by the affection in their voice and by the stories they tell. When you find a dog parent who is obviously crazy about his dog, pay attention to the recommendation.

Then ask some specific questions:

- Does the vet focus only on Western medicine, or does the vet have a more holistic practice? A veterinarian who is open to more healing methods than simply drugs and surgery will give your dog better care.

- Does the vet listen to the dog parent's concerns and input, or is the vet dismissive of input? You don't want a vet who thinks she knows all the answers or who discounts your instincts about your dog.

- Is the vet caring and patient with the animals? Is the vet's staff compassionate?

How is the vet with follow-up? Will he call to check on a dog after a serious procedure or illness?

Is the vet available for emergencies?

If the answers to your questions suggest that a vet is a possibility, make an appointment and take your dog to see the doctor. Watch how the vet interacts with your dog. Ask questions about how the vet would handle various common health problems.

Look around at the facilities. Are they clean? Does the staff seem happy? Does the place have an upbeat feel or a sad, miserable feel? Use your instincts. If you get any kind of bad feeling about a vet or clinic, walk away.

Sometimes You Need to Change Horses, Uh, Docs

Sometimes, even when you've asked all the right questions, and you think you've made a good choice, you may find that a vet stops giving the care your dog needs. You may discover new information, or the vet may start slipping for some reason.

I've talked to people who won't change vets because they don't want to hurt the vet's feelings. Forget the vet's feelings. It's your dog that matters. If you need to switch vets, switch vets.

Your dog deserves nothing less. When your dog has to have surgery, you don't want just any nincompoop putting her under anesthesia. When she needs medication, you don't want just any idiot prescribing something that could do her more harm than good. And no matter what kind of care she needs, you don't want her in the hands of someone who's just in it for the money or is burned out and doesn't give a darn about anything anymore. You want your dog in the hands of someone who cares and cares deeply, no matter how tired or overworked that person might be. You also want your dog in the hands of someone who's accessible, no matter what day of the week it is.

The Wrong Vet Can Kill

Too many people tend to see veterinary care as something they fit in when they have a chance. This attitude can kill.

I have a friend whom I love and who usually has good judgment about most things. However, she had a little dog that had been acting oddly for a couple of weeks. The dog could no longer jump up on the furniture, and she was coughing a lot. My friend had other worries—her father was dying. So she put off taking the dog to the vet. By the time she did, the vet told her the dog had fluid in her lungs and she needed to be put down.

Just like that. No second opinion. No valiant effort. Just give the dog a shot and put her down.

This same friend chose the vet because he was cheaper than the one I recommended and also closer. Cost and convenience. These things are more important than a dog's health, happiness, and their very life?

Of course, you need to consider cost and convenience when you choose a vet, but quality of care must come first. If you want your dog to live a long, healthy life, make sure she is in the hands of a quality vet.

When Your Vet Isn't Enough

No matter how good your vet is, sometimes you'll need more. You'll need specialty advice. Just as you wouldn't expect your general practitioner to repair your torn rotator cuff, you can't expect your vet to be able to solve your dog's more serious problems.

Dizzy developed obvious joint problems when she was only five years old. When it became apparent that walking was painful for her, I took her to the vet. The vet suggested I take her to a specialist. Some veterinarians are certified to specialize in areas like cardiology, neurology, ophthalmology, oncology, or orthopedics. I drove an hour and a half to an orthopedic veterinarian and paid for a full work-up. The verdict was that she had arthritis, and the only thing to do was to control it with steroids and aspirin. Not exactly what I wanted to hear—it was what my regular vet had been doing. But at least now I knew we were doing the best we could for her.

Renaldo Fischer's bulldog, Faccia Bello, had so many health problems that soon the dog had a "medical chart at the hospital . . . two inches thick," Fischer writes in *The Shaman Bulldog*. At one point, the vet informed Fischer that Faccia Bello needed plastic surgery. "You are surely kidding me," Fischer said. No, the vet explained, Faccia Bello's forehead skin folds were pushing the dog's eyelashes against the lenses of his eye, causing chronic pain and irritation. Nothing could cure this except correcting the source of the irritation. "So," says Fischer, "Faccia Bello had a radical facelift."

My parents' dog, Mickey, had surgery a few years ago on both his back legs to repair his anterior cruciate ligaments. The surgery cost $4,000. The specialist who performed the surgery is three hours away. The recovery time was over four months. When my parents, concerned about how they'd come up with the money on their fixed retirement income, spoke to a friend, the friend advised my parents not to have the surgery done. The expense and inconvenience were just too much. "You can't think of your dog as a member of the family," the friend said. "You must think of him as simply a pet."

Dog parents like my parents can't and won't do that. Your dog isn't simply a pet. Your dog is your child. So get your dog the specialty care she needs when she needs it.

Manipulation, Needles, Homeopathy, Oh My

Today, a variety of alternative veterinary care is available, including herbs, homeopathy, acupuncture, and chiropractic care. In Baker City, Oregon, a dachshund named Freedom severely injured his back. An injury that might have otherwise resulted in euthanasia was greatly improved by a chiropractor who had experience treating animals. Says Freedom's dog parent, the chiropractor gave Freedom "a new 'leash' on life."

Acupuncture can work similar miracles. The International Veterinary Acupuncture Society has more than 500 members nationwide. A couple of years ago, Muggins became terribly ill. At first, she was misdiagnosed with pancreatitis, and after surgery and several pricey tests, we were told her old inflammatory bowel disease was the cause of her suffering. Muggins was one miserable pup, and all the medicine we were giving her wasn't making her feel better. So I did a little research, and I found Dr. Patti Schaefer.

Dr. Schaefer practices in Olympia, Washington, which is an hour and a half away from us, but we happily made the drive. Dr. Schaefer did acupuncture on Muggins, and she advised us on nutrition changes and herbal therapies. These treatments worked like magic to transform our suffering pup into a happy dog again.

Muggins now gets regular acupuncture treatments from our local vet. In addition to helping with Muggins's inflammatory condition, the acupuncture has helped her hearing. Muggins isn't as young as she used to be, and when we noticed she was getting hard of hearing, we mentioned it to our vet. He tested the meridians (energy centers) in her ears and found they were blocked. With a couple of needles positioned properly in her ears, her hearing improved by over 50 percent.

Our local vet also uses homeopathy in his practice, and homeopathic remedies have done wonders for Muggins as well. One of the symptoms of her illness is nausea. She licks the air when she's nauseous, and for a while she licked the air constantly. It broke my heart to know how she was suffering. Other vets attempted to manage this with medications, none of which was helpful. When we first brought Muggins to her new vet and told him about her nausea, he knew just what to do. He prescribed a type of homeopathy that greatly reduced her symptoms. In combination with herbs, homeopathy has reduced Muggins's nausea by over 90 percent. She rarely licks the air anymore.

If I'd known about these therapies years ago, I'd have gotten more help for Dizzy. I would have located a veterinary chiropractor. I would have tried magnetic therapy, acupuncture, or massage. Money isn't an object. Effort is not a problem. Inconvenience is irrelevant.

When your dog is having health problems, be sure you explore all options for healing. Books on alternative therapies for dogs are available. You can find a list of alternative practitioners online at the Open Directory Project (*http://dmoz.org/Health/Animal/Alternative_Medicine/ Practitioners*), or you can do an online search for the specific therapy you're considering.

Your dog deserves the best care you can provide her. Dogs can't choose their vets. They don't even like vets and don't know enough to realize that they need those nasty people who poke sharp things into their skin, give them foul tasting stuff, and stick things up their behinds. Dogs don't know how to care for themselves in this way. You, as a dog parent, must do it for them. And if you're going to do it, doesn't it make sense that you should do it right?

chapter 11

Giving Your Dog Massages

In his book *A Dog Is Listening*, Roger Caras reminds us that parents cuddle their young and that "a good snuggle/cuddle provides parent and child with some of the best quality time we have." Caras says, "Dogs like to cuddle with their master, too." Okay, so he said, "master," but he's got the right idea. Dog parents know this. You love to cuddle your dogs. Dogs love to be rubbed and scratched, and good dog parents oblige.

Even dog *owners* pet their dogs. It's kind of a natural thing to stroke a dog, rub her belly, scratch her behind the ears, or simply pat her on the head or the rump. I've seen many owners of large dogs rub the dog's belly with their foot when the dog flops on her back near where the owner is standing.

Most people, though, pet their dogs like they're petting a dog. They stroke them or scratch them. They don't massage them. Dog parents massage their dogs.

Ooh, Aah, That Feels Good

Massaging a dog is different from petting one. Have you ever had a Swedish massage, the kind where the masseuse kneads the skin and muscles until you're absolutely purring? That's massage. To massage a dog, you have to work their skin and muscles in kneading strokes just like you'd like your spouse to do to you.

Start at your dog's shoulders and work your way slowly down her back to her rump. Spread out your fingers and work them into your dog's fur, all the way to the skin, exerting enough pressure to reach beneath to the muscle. Be gentle but firm (kind of like the way you have to be when disciplining a dog). At this point, if your dog likes what you're doing, she will usually stick her nose up in the air. It's her way of saying, "Oh, yeah!" If you stop the massage, your dog will probably nose you, her way of saying, "No, don't stop."

Move your hands slowly over your dog, kneading and rolling and pressing, until you get to her rump. Be a little more firm there because the muscle is thicker and tougher. Then work your way down your dog's flanks.

Some dogs don't like you to mess with their feet, but some, like Muggins, love to have the pads of their feet massaged. You can also massage the sides of your dog's mouth and under her chin. Gather your dog's ears up and rub them between your fingers. This will probably send her nose even higher up into the air.

If you really want to get creative and thorough about giving your dog a massage, check out the book *Dog Massage,* by Maryjean Ballner. Ballner suggests experimenting with different techniques to see which ones your dog likes. You can always tell what feels good to dogs. I've found several types of massage that Muggins enjoys.

Keep Making Little Circles

On Muggins's belly, I use a technique called Tellington Touch. Linda Tellington created this form of massage specifically for animals. The method is said to decrease stress and tension and help with behavior problems. Tellington and her associates offer workshops teaching the techniques, and many animal behaviorists are trained to use the method.

The basic stroke is a circular motion using firm pressure from the tips of the first three fingers. You use the stroke over and over, moving your fingers to a different spot on the animal each time. You repeat that circular pattern, covering the entire animal this way.

Try this if your animal is in a lot of pain or is anxious for any reason. The stroke tends to be calming to most dogs. I've helped Muggins through a lot of pain using this stroke.

Morning, Noon and Night

Any time is a good time to massage your dog. Mornings, however, are especially good. You know how you're often stiff in the morning. Your dog is too, especially if she is older. Help your dog get going in the morning by giving her a little massage.

Massage is a great way to greet your dog in the morning, too. It's a wonderful way to express your love.

I usually do some version of massage on Muggins in the morning when we first wake up. It's my way of greeting Muggins and letting her know I'm happy to see her and happy to have her with me at the start of my day. She, in turn, licks my face and hands as her way of telling me she's happy to be with me, too.

Morning isn't the only time I massage Muggins, though. I try and give her little massages, even if for only a few seconds, every time I sit down to cuddle and pet her. I know it feels good to her, and I believe it helps keep her healthy. Massage increases circulation and helps remove toxins from the system. Given the kinds of disgusting things that dogs love to eat (like crab shells, horse manure, bugs, and the like), I think removing toxins is an important thing to do.

With Massage, You Can Heel, Uh, Heal

Massage can also heal major ailments. When Satin, a twelve-year-old rottweiler, developed osteoporosis and such severe arthritis that her hind legs dragged when she walked, her dog parent took her to a shiatsu (a Japanese technique that focuses on pressure points on the body) massage practitioner. According to an article, "Woof! That Feels Good . . . " by Norine Dworkin, in the October 2000 issue of *Good Housekeeping*, Satin was running around on all fours again within a few months.

If your dog is having major joint or muscle pain, talk to your vet about finding a massage practitioner who works on dogs. You can also look up "Massage" in the Yellow Pages and talk to the practitioners directly. Some have experience with animals.

The Touch of Love

The massages you give your dogs are definitely good for them. But massage will do even more for your dog. Massage will make your dog feel special. I know it makes Muggins feel special. The sideways glance of her eyes tells me that she recognizes the touch as her due because she is so sure of my love for her.

Touch is a universal language. Whether the language is dog, cat, Chinese, Russian, or English, a hug is a hug, a gentle touch is a gentle touch, a punch is a punch, and a massage is a massage. Massage provides your dogs with comfort, but it also communicates love. Sharing one body's energy with another's is the hands and heart of one person saying to another, "You are important; you are a divine being and I honor you." When you massage your dog, this is the message you give her. It reassures her.

Massage your dog when your dog is frightened or hurt. The touch will be soothing and comforting.

One day, a wasp got stuck in the folds of Muggins's jowls and stung her so badly that her muzzle on that side swelled to four times its normal size. Muggins whimpered her misery. I applied a baking soda paste and an icepack for as long as she'd tolerate it, but when she squirmed free of the first aid, I just sat with her and massaged her until she calmed and eventually went to sleep. The massage eased her pain and gave her comfort.

As a dog parent, it's your job to give your dog comfort. It's also your joy. You get that joy from your dog's easy breathing and from those little doggy groans that are your dog's way of purring. These are reward enough, don't you think?

chapter 12

Buying Furniture with Your Dog in Mind

hen I was growing up, Shorty wasn't allowed on most of the furniture in our house. She could only get up on one end of the sofa in the family room, where Mom had spread out a towel to protect the upholstery from Shorty's hair and the other dirty things Shorty might leave behind.

I always wished Shorty was allowed on all the furniture because I wanted to cuddle her no matter where I was sitting. I fervently wished she could have slept in my bed at night, but my parents were dog owners then. They hadn't yet learned to be dog parents, and they thought dogs belonged on the floor.

When I got Dizzy, I encouraged her to get up on all the soft furniture. Of course, things like tables and desks were off-limits. I wanted her on the sofas, the chairs, and the bed. I wanted her near me, and I wanted her to be comfortable. She was happy to oblige.

My parents also relaxed their standards when they got their next dog, Corki. Corki was allowed, even encouraged, to be on all the soft furniture. Mom and Dad were becoming dog parents.

A dog allowed on the furniture is a happy dog, a comfortable dog. She's a dog who's included in the family

life, and she knows she's included. That inclusion is very
important to dogs.

Not All Furniture Is Created Equal

Given that having your dogs on the furniture is good for
human and canine comfort, as a dog parent, you need to
take steps to make sure that your furniture is not only
human-friendly, but canine-friendly as well. When you purchase your furniture, at least your soft furniture—things
like sofas, easy chairs, and beds—you need to do so with
your dog in mind.

Have you ever watched a dog try and get comfortable
on a piece of furniture unsuited to dogs? The dog looks a bit
confused—like she should be enjoying lying on this people-
sofa but she doesn't like how it feels. A dog tries to rest her
chin on the arm of a sofa, but the arm is too high and her chin
keeps sliding off. A big dog invited up onto a loveseat that's
too narrow struggles to keep her legs on the furniture.

For your dog's comfort, you need to keep a few things
in mind when you purchase furniture. The arm of the seats
must be padded and low. You don't want your dog to have to
rest her chin on hard wood. You don't want your dog to get
neck strain trying to make do with an arm that's too high.

The seat of the furniture must be roomy enough to
accommodate your dog. If you have a small dog, you don't
need to worry much, but larger dogs obviously require
larger furniture. Don't cheat your dog out of her comfort by
getting stingy with furniture size. If you intend to share the
furniture with your dog, you need to consider space. Easy
chairs need extra-wide seats so your dog can curl up next

to you. Sofas need to be long enough to allow you to stretch out and still have your dog by your feet.

The top of the back of the sofa is important too. Many dogs, Muggins included, enjoy draping themselves over the top of the back of a sofa. If the sofa is in front of a window, this is especially true. Dogs need a wide, cushy place to perch their chest and front legs while they watch the world go by. Some dogs, like Muggins, enjoy lying on top of the back of sofas like a cat would do. A wide, stable area is required for this.

Size is important in purchasing beds as well. Even if you're single, you need a large bed. You must give your dog room to sprawl out, and it's nice if you have room to sprawl out yourself even when your dog is sprawled out. King-sized beds are ideal. They're essential, in fact, if you have multiple dogs and/or cats or if you sleep with a human companion.

Your furniture's color and fabric are also important. Even though you want your dogs on the furniture, you don't want your house to look like the inside of a barn. Choosing a color that won't show the dirt your dog might track in is important. Trying to also choose a color that won't show the dog hair can be challenging, but it's worth the trouble if you want to keep your home presentable. Leather or vinyl furniture is generally a bad idea. These surfaces are entirely unfair to your dog. They're cold on their bellies, not to mention slippery and totally uninviting. If you do have leather or vinyl, you must cover it with something soft. Dogs can make do with afghans and throws.

A Place for Your Head

I haven't always known all these bits of wisdom about buying furniture. I've made mistakes in the past. My first sofa had high arms, and Dizzy often slept with her neck craned and her nose pointed up in the air. The living-room furniture in my last house had a narrow back so that Muggins was continually falling off of it. The fabric was pale cream-colored, and it showed the dirt so badly that I constantly had to tell Muggins to get off the sofa when her feet were wet.

When I bought my new house, however, I purchased the furniture entirely for Muggins's comfort. The salesperson thought I was totally out of my mind. She was talking early American or contemporary, and I was talking canine. I didn't care a whit what she thought of me, though. What mattered was what Muggins would think.

I can tell what Muggins thinks every time she lies down, heaves a contented sigh, and settles her chin on the padded, low arm of the sofa. I can tell whenever she drapes herself over the soft, broad top of the sofa to look out the window or stretches out on the top of the sofa to watch me cook dinner.

What also matters is what I think. I think it's great that Muggins is sprawled near my feet while I'm watching television. I think it's wonderful to have her nestled against my belly when I'm curled on my side with a book. I think it's terrific that I can only see that the furniture is covered with white dog hair and dirt if I lean close to inspect the fabric. I think having a dog on the furniture is one of the great joys of life, and being a good dog parent means having furniture that's perfectly suited to your dog.

chapter 13

Comfortable Sleeping Places
All Around the House

Even after you've purchased your furniture with your dog in mind, you still have more to do to ensure your dog's sleeping and resting comfort. As great as your furniture might be for your dog, you're not always in a room where the dog has access to that furniture. Therefore, dog parents can never have too many dog beds. No matter how many you have, you always wish you had more. Or at least your dog does.

We've domesticated dogs. We've taken them out of the wild. We've turned them into our furry kids. We've softened them up—in effect, we've turned them into canine princes and princesses who must be treated accordingly.

I mean, can you really expect little Fifi to sleep on the floor? Would you expect your child to sleep on the floor? Dogs have feelings, too. They have muscles, bones, and spinal cords that need cushioned support. Your prince or princess needs soft places to lie. Dog beds provide those soft places.

Here a Bed, There a Bed

Notice that I said soft places, plural. You need several dog beds because you spend a lot of time in several places in your house. Your dog needs a bed in your bedroom, even if she usually sleeps on the bed with you. This gives your dog the choice of sleeping on the ground.

That's what dog beds are for—it's all about choice. For example, I have a loveseat in my office for Muggins to lie on, positioned where she can look out the window. But it's about six feet from my desk—too far away to suit her sometimes. So I put the dog bed on the floor near my chair. When she was a puppy, she liked to be even closer. She wanted to be next to my feet under the desk. It was hard and cold under there because I had a plastic carpet protector under the desk and chair. So I bought another bed, a small one with an eight-inch high back. That let Muggins curl up by my feet.

Your dog would love to have a cozy den in every room where you spend a lot of time. Give your dog what she'd love. As Chapter 6 explains in its discussion of the importance of giving your dog a view, if your dog needs to lie on the floor to see out the window, place a dog bed in that position.

You also need a dog bed for outside if your dog spends time lying outdoors. Muggins loves to lie outside and keep an eye on her backyard. When I put the pad on the lounge chair in the summer months, she stretched out on that. In the winter, after I took the pad inside, she went back to lying on the deck. I realized that she needed something soft to lie on outside, and I got another dog bed. I put it out in the morning and bring it in at night. Muggins loves it. She often spends hours in the evenings sprawled out on her dog bed, settled in where she can keep an eye on me resting in the living room.

You can get dog beds that are water and sun resistant. These are perfect for outside locations.

Canines in Waiting

Dogs spend an enormous amount of their time sleeping. They spend an even more enormous amount of time lying around watching you, hanging around nearby while you do your thing. They wait patiently while you read, watch television, work, or talk on the phone. They settle by your feet. They sit as close as possible to watch you cook dinner. They live their lives around you. Much of their lives is spent waiting.

Canines in waiting deserve some comfort. Providing a few cushy places for a dog to lie while the dog does her doggy waiting isn't much to ask of a good dog parent.

So Many Choices

Dog beds don't cost that much. Yeah, you can spend a bundle on a designer canine couch. You can get cedar-chip-filled, flannel-covered, premier dog beds. If you can afford it, go for it. But if you can't, a simple canvas-covered fiberfill will do nicely. As long as it's soft and big enough for your dog to stretch out if and when she wants, almost any bed is acceptable. You can even use old pillows, blankets, bed-spreads, or down comforters as beds. As a bonus, you'll find these quite inexpensively at any secondhand store.

If you don't have room on your bed or your sofa for your dog, you need dog beds. If your sofas are hard or made of leather or otherwise uncomfortable for your dog, you need dog beds. Every room in the house, every place where you spend time and where your dog therefore waits for you, should have a comfortable, soft spot for your dog to rest while waiting.

This isn't to say that if you provide your dog with these spots, she'll necessarily choose to use them. Right now, Muggins is stretched out on the floor behind my office chair. The dog bed and the loveseat are empty. The point, however, is that she has the choice. If she chooses to sit on the floor, that's fine, but I want her to have the option of something softer if she needs it.

She's been waiting for two hours for me to get off the computer and go do something more fun. Placing a little bit of softness at her disposal gives her access to comfort in the meantime.

chapter 14

Letting Your Dog Call the Shots Once in Awhile

Human beings have a tendency to think that dogs should be at their beck and call. Even dog parents are guilty of this attitude from time to time. You feed your dog when you decide it's feeding time. You walk the dog when it fits into your schedule. You play when you want to play.

Sometimes this is necessary. You have a household to run, a job to hold, and possibly a family to raise. Your dog can't control your every action. But you can sometimes let your dog be the boss.

The Best Seat In The House

I have a reasonably small house. My living room holds only two pieces of furniture suitable for sitting—a sofa and a loveseat. My favorite place to sit is on the sofa, with my legs stretched out the length of the sofa and my back against a large teddy bear that sits at the end. From this position, I can easily see the television. I'm propped up for reading, and I'm sprawled out for maximum comfort. This is "the good spot" in my living room.

If I had my way, while I was resting in the good spot, Muggins would lie on the sofa near my feet. Or if she wanted to sprawl out or rest her head against the left arm of a sofa, she could lie on the loveseat, which sits at a right angle to the sofa. Tim likes to sit on the loveseat, and Muggins can lie next to him. This is the way it often works . . . *if* I can beat her to the good spot. The truth is, Muggins loves the spot against the big bear as much as I do. She loves to curl up and rest her chin on the bear's legs. So she and I often vie for that spot on the sofa.

If she gets to the spot before I do or steals it when I get up, I don't move her. As a good dog parent, I know one of the ways I can give Muggins comfort is by letting her be where she wants to be, even if she has taken *my* place on the furniture.

If I get the spot before Muggins does, she begins her cute canine campaign for the good spot. She often starts with an aggrieved sigh as she settles down on the loveseat, looking put out. Or if it's nice enough outside, she'll lie on the dog bed out on the deck just outside the sliding glass door. Eventually, though, she comes to me where I'm reclining happily against the bear. She either sits down next to me on the floor or jumps up and stands in my lap. Then she stares at me.

She just stares.

Jowls hanging forward, little creases bunched up between her eyebrows. Ears at a half-prick. Eyes intent. Staring.

I don't need to read a book on how to communicate with animals to understand what she's saying: *Move. I want your spot.*

Unfortunately, even if I outlast the stares, I usually come up against another problem. Eventually, I have to pee. This requires getting up. Once I get up, it's all over. I've lost my spot.

I ignore my bladder as long as possible while Muggins continues to stare and/or sigh. Finally, though, I must give in to my body's insistence. When I come back into the room, Muggins is lying against the teddy bear, her chin on its leg. She looks up at me out of the corner of her eye as if to say, "I knew you'd give it up eventually."

Who says humans get dibs on the good seats? We're bigger? We paid for them? Personally, I don't think these are very good reasons to deprive your dog of her comfort. Yes, I know Muggins would be just as comfortable on the loveseat. It's not exactly a hardship for her to be in a different spot. But the good spot makes her happy. She's comfortable in that spot. In return for all the happiness and comfort she brings me, giving up my spot to her now and then is a small thing to give back.

I have a friend who has actually slept in the spare room sometimes because her dog would push her out of her spot on the bed, and she wouldn't move the dog. She didn't want to disturb her dog's sleep. Her husband did the same thing if the dog pushed him out of his spot.

This is one of the ways you can let your dog call the shots—let your dog have the good spot on the furniture once in awhile. Let your dog sleep where she wants to sleep once in awhile. It's not going to kill you to give up your favorite place from time to time.

I'm Hungry NOW

If you're like a lot of dog parents, and if you don't let your dog graze on dry food throughout the day, you probably have a regular doggy feeding time. There's nothing inherently wrong with this. However, dogs are like humans in that their hunger needs vary. Some days they get hungry earlier than others.

Muggins always comes to tell me when she's hungry. She comes and either whines at me in a particular way or she noses my leg then trots into the kitchen. Sometimes she paws at her feeding station.

A great way to let your dog call the shots is to let your dog tell you when she wants to eat. You can easily tell when your dog is hungry. Pay attention. Unless you're gone all day and have only one or two times available for feeding your dog, be open to feeding at different times. When you're a dog parent, you're in tune with your dog. When your dog lets you know she's hungry, go ahead and feed her, even if it isn't your prescribed feeding time.

Let's Play NOW

We've already talked about playing the way your dog wants to. You also need to play when your dog wants to.

Don't wait until the end of the day, when you've finished everything you need to get done. If you do that, you're likely to never play with your dog. Playing will be the afterthought you don't get to.

It neither takes much time nor causes much inconvenience to stop and play with your dog for a few minutes when your dog wants to play. Now, of course, you might have a problem if your dog wants to play constantly. Even then, though, you can sometimes make accommodations.

I had a friend who told me you should never let a dog take the alpha, or top dog, positioning in your family. You should never, he said, let your dog call the shots because then your dog will walk all over you.

I haven't found that to be the case. When you give your dog a little control, you're giving your dog a form of comfort. In the end, you make the rules, and you'll do things mostly in your time and in your way. But if you can't move your butt out of the way once in awhile so your dog can have her favorite warm place to lie, if you can't adjust your schedule to meet your dog's needs, then you're not doing a good job of making your canine happy. You're not doing your job as a good dog parent.

chapter 15

Grooming and Dressing Your Dog Well

Even dog owners usually brush their dogs and give their dogs the occasional bath. Dog parents, however, know that good grooming is essential to a comfortable dog. You learn early on how to clip your dog's nails, clean her ears, and brush her teeth. You know how to check for knotted fur between her toes and behind her ears between grooming. You know how to use moisturizing shampoos and conditioners to prevent dry skin. You even know how to do the not-so-fun things like express anal sacs.

Awhile back, my mother introduced me to her new neighbors. I was in my four-wheel-drive at the time, and I had Muggins with me. The man said hello to me then walked to the back window of the vehicle to say hello to Muggins. He reached in and scratched her ears. He spoke to her, and while he talked, he wiped the corners of her eyes. I knew immediately that he was a dog parent. Dog parents always wipe their dog's eyes when they notice they're dirty. My mother does it with a tissue. I do it with my fingers just as my mother's neighbor did. I do it dozens of times a day. It's a habit, something I do usually without thinking. Keeping a dog well-groomed is second nature to a good dog parent.

A Hair Cut Above

I tried for years to find a groomer whom I trusted to groom Muggins. Unfortunately, the choices I had available to me didn't make the cut.

As you do when you search for a good vet, to find a good groomer, you ask fellow dog parents for recommendations. When you get a recommendation, call the groomer and tell him you want to watch him groom your dog the first time. If the groomer won't agree, find another groomer. You have a right to watch how the groomer interacts with your dog. You want a groomer who will treat your dog gently.

A good groomer also needs to listen. You don't want a groomer who thinks she knows how your dog should be trimmed. You know what your dog needs, and you want a groomer who will follow your directions.

The grooming facility must be clean and well kept. If you take a flea-free dog to a groomer and your dog comes home with fleas, find another groomer. Fleas are abundant enough—you shouldn't have to pay to invite some home for dinner.

Don't ever take your dog to a groomer who smokes in the grooming facility. Your dog deserves to breathe fresh air. (If you smoke yourself, please think about what the habit is doing to your dog. Dogs can be harmed by second-hand smoke.)

If You Want It Done Right, Do It Yourself

After subjecting Muggins to several not-so-clean-looking places and having her fur shaved too close or left too long, and even having her come home with cuts behind her ears once in awhile, I finally decided to learn to groom her myself. I bought a good pair of clippers and some scissors, and taught myself how to groom her. I've become pretty good at it, and I know that at least she's in good hands.

You can find good, reasonably priced clippers in any discount pet catalog. Look for clippers advertised as "quiet" because your dog won't like a loud buzz, especially near her ears. Look for clippers with several comb attachments so you can choose the length to which you want to cut the fur. You can also buy instructional videos for clipping. I suggest you watch one, and then just dive in. You'll get better at it every time you do it.

Canine Couture

The extent of a canine's need for fashion depends on the dog, of course, but the bare minimum required is a collar and an identification (ID) tag. Years ago, a collar was a collar. Not anymore. You go into any pet store or flip through any pet supply catalog and you see a myriad of collars in styles, materials and colors that boggle the mind. Pretty much anything goes. Some collars even have semiprecious stones set into them.

Even if you don't have the kind of money that would allow you to buy your dog such fancy collars, you can indulge in collars that have unique colors or patterns.

Muggins looks particularly fine in red. So I like to get her collars with red patterns.

The collar should have two tags—a license and an ID tag. You probably don't like to imagine any situations in which your dog might get separated from you, but if let's say you had an accident and became unconscious. The license and ID will keep your dog out of a shelter.

You can also consider having a microchip put in your dog. Talk to your vet about doing this. The procedure is quick and although not quite painless, it's not much worse than a shot. The microchip contains digital information that can be read by a special scanner. Once the microchip is inserted, the number will be on file, along with your identifying information. If your dog is ever lost and also loses her collar, the people who find your dog will be able to find you.

Accessories Complete a Look

In addition to her collars, I have a couple other accessories for Muggins. I have three collar covers, material sewn in a narrow tube with elastic at both ends. The tube is slid over the collar, scrunching up the material as it goes, so the effect is a bunched up bandana around the dog's neck. It's a natty look that's easy to achieve and stays perfectly in place.

Muggins also occasionally wears bandanas, but she's not that thrilled with them. She shakes a bit more often when she's wearing one, as if she'd like to get the thing off of her. I usually put them on her only for special occasions like her birthday or Christmas. Many people these days have bandanas on their dogs most of the time. Dogs look great in bandanas.

Then there's the headgear available for dogs. Many styles of hats are available with holes for the dog's ears and a tie or strap to go under her chin to hold the hat in place. Last Christmas, I bought Muggins a Santa hat that had strings that slipped over her ears and tied under her neck. She wasn't thrilled with it. But she went along. Made for a great picture.

Some dogs wear sunglasses. Some dogs wear jewelry. You can get pendants in all sorts of metals to hang from your dog's collar. Muggins used to have one made, thankfully, just from stainless steel. It had a heart surrounded by angel wings on it—I got it for her because I call her "my angel dog." The metal eventually wore out, though, and it fell off her collar. I found it lying on the deck. There is some risk to canine jewelry.

Even so, just because a dog already has a fur coat doesn't mean she can't use a little finery. Dogs may not be as obsessed with their appearance as humans are, but they still have a little vanity. Muggins seems to know that when she's wearing one of the collar sleeves, she's looking hot. She prances a bit more, holds her head a bit higher.

Baby, It's Cold Outside— How About a Coat?

Many dogs, like Muggins, are bred for sport and water. These dogs have their own coat to keep them warm on even the coldest days. The fur on these dogs was meant to get wet. This is why I've never felt compelled to dress Muggins in a sweater or coat.

As Dizzy got older, on the other hand, she sometimes needed the protection of a coat. When she developed a thyroid condition that left her fur sparse and exposed the skin on her back, she got especially cold on rainy days. So I bought her a doggy raincoat.

If you're not sure whether or not your dog needs a sweater or coat, ask your vet for advice. Your vet will know which breeds tolerate the elements and which breeds don't. You can also just observe your dog in bad weather. Is she shivering? Is she sneezing? Does she look uncomfortable? Dogs communicate a lot more than most people give them credit for. Pay attention to your dog's comfort level, and that will tell you what you need to buy.

Just because your dog needs a coat, though, doesn't mean she'll like it when you get it for her. Dizzy hated the raincoat I bought her. It was adorable, of course. It was light blue and had a little hood that came up over her head. The whole time she wore it, she had an expression of abject embarrassment that deepened whenever we encountered another dog. Her attitude was, "I'm so mortified that they're making me wear this thing." Brad said he was sure Dizzy thought the coat made her appear wimpy. Perhaps she did think that. All I know is that the coat kept her dry and warm.

The man I occasionally encounter on the beach who has the two miniature schnauzers (one male, one female), dresses the dogs in knit sweaters on cold days and raincoats on very rainy days. The male wears blue and the female wears red or pink. They're adorable, but more important, they're warm.

For Those Special Occasions

I once met a woman whose golden retriever was the ring-bearer in a wedding. For the occasion, the dog wore a home-made tuxedo. The woman said he stole the show from the bride and groom. I'm sure he did. What could be cuter than a dog wearing a tux?

Once a year, the town I live in hosts a weekend for motorcyclists. Motorcycle enthusiasts set up booths of clothing and biking paraphernalia. The clothing booths inevitably include little leather jackets for dogs. One year, I saw one of the jackets on a pug. Talk about canine style.

Have you ever noticed dogs preening a bit after they've had their bath? Dogs get it—they understand that they're looking good, and they play it to the hilt. A salesperson at Dog-O-Rama, a clothing boutique for dogs in New York City, says, "[Dogs] have a sense that they're a person and should dress up like a person."

A well-dressed dog is a happy dog. A well-dressed dog is a safe dog. A well-dressed dog is a healthy dog. All of this makes for a comfortable dog. As a dog parent, you must not only pay attention to the details of grooming, you must also keep your dogs dressed in style.

chapter 16

Having Healthy Treats Handy at All Times

Good parents reward their kids for good behavior. They also provide treats just for fun. A good dog parent does the same. As I've noted, though, dogs are different than kids. Dogs can learn, but you can't reason with them. Because of this, treats take on an even more important role in dog parenting.

When you get a puppy, you quickly realize that dog treats are an essential part of creating a dog you can live with. Although there are ways to train dogs without treats— dogs can be trained with lots of praise, for example—most training programs suggest giving your dog a treat every time they do something you want them to do.

I'll Do It for a Treat

Most dogs are highly motivated by treats. They will work diligently to figure out what you want from them just for the simple reward of a small treat and a little bit of praise.

When I got Dizzy, I knew nothing about training dogs. Nor did I know about proper canine nutrition (discussed in Chapter 9). But it didn't take me long to figure out that Dizzy would do pretty much anything in exchange for food. I trained her to sit, stay, and "give me five" (the doggy equivalent of a high-five) using potato chips as rewards. She learned all three commands within half an hour.

By the time I got Muggins, I knew more about nutrition and more about training. I got a supply of dog treats and set about training her. Again, the process was quick and easy. When she knew that a treat was forthcoming, she worked hard to do what I wanted her to do.

After I taught Muggins the basics, I found other uses for treats—so many uses, in fact, that I saw a need to have a wide variety of treats. I figured it was bad enough that dogs have to eat the same food day after day; they don't need to be stuck with the same treats as well. Unfortunately, I found out that all those treats weren't so good for Muggins. Many of them were too high in fat, and they exacerbated her inflammatory bowel condition. I learned an important lesson—dogs can get too much of a good thing.

Muggins now gets only two types of treats. She either gets a small bite of chicken, or she gets a couple of prescription diet kibbles.

I still use the treats to encourage her, though. For instance, I give her a treat for doing things she doesn't like to do. I want her to know that she will be rewarded for going along with things she's not crazy about. It tends to foster a bit more canine cooperation. After her bath, after having her nails clipped or her ears cleaned, after taking medications, or after anything she doesn't enjoy, she gets a treat.

You can make your training a lot easier if you use treats as rewards when you train. Punishment does not help a dog learn. Reward does.

Treats Just Because

Then there are the other times a dog can get a treat. After going outside for the last time before bed, your dog could get a treat. Sometimes your dog will just decide that it's time for a treat. Muggins, for instance, will sometimes just romp into the kitchen, bark a couple times and look at the refrigerator in such an adorable way that she gets a bite of chicken for her trouble. (Of course, there's no purpose in giving her a treat in this situation. It's simply evidence that I'm even better trained than she is.)

Muggins gets two enzyme tablets after she eats her meals, and to her, these are treats. It's her version of dessert. When she has finished her meal, she finds me, no matter where I am in the house. She expects her "dessert nummies." And she gets them. Then she burps, wags her tail, and wanders off in search of a toy.

I keep a bag of kibble on the floor in my truck as well. As I mentioned in Chapter 7, Muggins gets a treat when she spots a horse, a cow, a dog, a cat, a deer or a person on a bicycle, and she gets a treat when I come back out to the car after running errands.

She's also managed to finagle a treat for barking at the golf course we pass between the beach and home. After observing her bark at the same area every day for weeks, I finally concluded she must be responding to the smell of goose droppings because geese hang out on the fairway. So now she gets a treat for barking at goose poop.

Heck, she gets a treat when she stares at the bag long enough for me to forget myself and give her one just because she asked for it. As I say, I'm well-trained.

Dogs believe that it is their God-given right to get treats. Dogs think they ought to get treats just because they're as cute as all get out. Whether or not dogs ought to get treats just for breathing, they do—if you're a good dog parent.

Of course giving your dogs treats can be overdone. As I found out the hard way, you can give too many treats and create an unhealthy dog. But not if you're careful. If you use kibble as treats, each bite is small. As long as I don't hand out too many, I'm not hurting my dog, and the cost is minimal.

The payback, however, is huge. The payback is a happy dog, one that actually does what you want her to do most of the time. For the price of a few treats, you get a dog that trusts you and greets you with a wag.

Yeah, I know. They'd do that anyway. That's what dogs do. But great dog parents enjoy rewarding their dogs for being themselves. In the process, you reward yourself. Not a bad treat for all concerned.

chapter 17

Sleeping with Your Dog

It's 2:30 in the morning. I'm lost in a haze of sleep, aware only of the dreams playing out on the stage of my subconscious mind. The bed shifts, and I feel the tug of consciousness. Now I'm aware of the firm mattress supporting me, the warm covers cocooning my body, and something else. . . .

Again, I feel the bed shift, and a warm heaviness plops down on the mattress, a weight of pure relaxation. The warmth presses against my back, solid, yet soft. I hear a long sigh, the smacking of jowls, a quiet groan. I smile.

I press back against that warmth cuddling up to me, and I let myself drift back to sleep knowing that all is well. This is one of the best parts of being a dog parent—sleeping with your dog.

Puppies and Fidgeters Need Not Apply

Sleeping with your dog is a great way to be a dog parent, and it's great fun, too. Sometimes, though, it really isn't possible. If a dog is going to disrupt your sleep or get into trouble by sleeping with you, you need to make other arrangements.

Muggins spent the first six months of her life sleeping in a dog crate. It was the only way for me and Brad to get a night's rest. As she grew, we started testing her, letting her sleep in a bed on the floor out of her crate as long as she stayed in the room and didn't wake us too early. If she tried to jump up and lick my face before I was ready to get up, I put her in her crate. She soon learned that if she wanted to avoid the crate she had to remain quiet until I greeted her, saying, "Good morning, Muggins." This was her cue that she could lick my face and start jumping around.

At this point, I would've been happy to invite Muggins into our bed for the whole night, but Brad thought it was too crowded. He complained about having his legs cramped into one position when a dog slept against him or feeling like he was being pushed out of the bed.

If you feel this way, you may not want your dog to sleep with you. That's okay. It doesn't make you a bad dog parent. But if you can't let your dog sleep with you, at least let your dog sleep near you. And give your dog a soft, comfortable place to lie by making sure a dog bed or blanket is on the floor by your bed.

The Joys of Nighttime and Morning Cuddling

About a year before Brad and I divorced, we separated for a couple months. Muggins and I went to live in a beach cottage at Cannon Beach. I brought along her bed but also gave her the option of joining me. She chose to join me. I was thrilled. Her body pressing against me kept me warm during the windy, rainy January and February nights on the coast. I loved the sound of her even breathing. I even sort of loved it when she stretched out in the middle of the night, pressed her paws firmly into my back and flexed her nails into my skin.

In the morning, when Muggins woke up, she would lie still and wait for me to greet her. She had remembered the lessons learned in puppyhood, and she rarely woke me up. Sometimes, though, when I slept too late, she'd reach out a paw and tap the pillow a few inches from my face. A gentle tap. No sound. Just a soft reminder that she was there and a day was waiting to be explored. I'd open my eyes, look at her and feel her tail thump against the bed, hear the whisper of fur against sheets. She'd stare at me intently, waiting.

"Good morning, Muggins."

She'd wag her tail even harder and squirm toward me to lick my face. I loved these morning greetings as much as having her warm presence in the bed at night.

I loved all this closeness so much that as soon as Brad and I split up for good, I welcomed Muggins into my bed. If you give your dog a chance to sleep with you, you might find that the pleasures and the positives outweigh the inconvenience and the negatives.

Sometimes in the night, you'll roll over and press up against your dog. Wrap an arm around her and soak in the sensation of soft fur and warm body, the comforting rhythm of rising and falling ribs, the breath of the life that you treasure. During those times, you might find yourself waking even further from sleep, rousing yourself so you can enjoy the magic of this connection in the dark silence of the night. This is great. Be filled with appreciation for having this comforting, eager presence in your bed, in your life.

If the Bed Doesn't Fit . . .

Sometimes the only reason your dog is a problem in your bed is your bed isn't big enough. That was the problem when Brad and I first got Dizzy. So we got a bigger bed, a queen size. Once we did that, Dizzy was welcome to join us at night.

I bought an even bigger bed for Muggins's and me—a king size. I wanted to make sure that if another man ever came into my life, there'd be plenty of room in the bed for man and canine. Good planning. Tim and I happily share the bed now with Muggins, who usually manages to get the lion's share of it.

If you can afford it and you have the room, get yourself a king-size bed. If you can't do that, how about putting a plush chair near your bed so your dog can sleep almost at your level and very close by? The chair doesn't have to stay there all day. I know a couple that pulls a chair from another part of the room and positions it near their bed every night. Their dog sleeps happily in the chair, and he feels like he's in bed with his parents.

The Sounds of Contentment

Last night, Muggins had her head on my pillow, her muzzle only an inch or so from my cheek. I could feel her breath against my skin, warm and even. I could have moved her. But why? That breath was as enjoyable as a soft caress.

After a few minutes, she started to dream—soft whuffs, whines, yips, and jowl smacks only a couple inches from my ear. She began to twitch, and the pillow vibrated. I smiled. The more she twitched and yipped, the more I smiled. I had my husband, the human love of my life, on one side of me and Muggins, my canine love, on the other. It doesn't get much better than this, I thought to myself.

If you're awakened by your dog's dreaming, please don't be annoyed. Listen for a few seconds. You'll hear the sounds of life, a blessed life that brings you much joy. Enjoy it.

Slugs Need Not Apply, Either

As Chapter 5 discusses in depth, dogs do get dirty. You can use a whisk broom to sweep off the sheets before you climb into bed if your dog has left little nature gifts under the covers.

About the only thing that tends to rattle me is when Muggins brings tiny baby slugs to bed. These she occasionally collects on her fur. Here I draw the line. Slugs are not welcome in my bed. So now I give Muggins the once-over before she comes to bed.

Dogs love sleeping in your bed. You may have to work your way up to it starting when your dog is still a puppy, but usually, by the time she's a year old, your dog can sleep in your bed without disrupting a thing. If you possibly can, let your dog sleep with you. Sharing a bed strengthens the bond between human and canine. That bond is the core of being a great dog parent.

How lovely that you can do some of your best dog-parenting while you sleep.

PART III: SECURITY

Dogs are dependent creatures. Their every action hinges on what you do. They live most of their lives waiting to see what you want from them, waiting to see what comes next. Because of the inherent uncertainty in their lives, they enjoy routine. It gives them security.

Everyone wants security—the knowledge that we're safe and that everything will be okay. Although even we humans can't always guarantee our own security, at least we have some control. Whatever security dogs have comes entirely from us. A good dog parent knows this.

It takes a little bit of thought and understanding of the canine psyche to provide a dog with security. If you're a good dog parent, you will, for example, talk to your dog a lot so the dog knows what will come next. You have a dog door in your home. You will rarely, if ever, kennel your dog. You will rarely, if ever, leave your dog tied up alone. As much as possible, when your dog wants attention, you will stop what you're doing and give her some love. You will include your dog in as much of your life as you can. You trust what your dog is communicating to you. You consider your dog's needs when making life decisions.

These small efforts to keep your dog in the loop of daily life gives her that sense of security she needs. You may not be able to control everything. But good dog parents do their best to give their dogs as secure a life as possible.

chapter 18

Talking to Your Dog, a Lot

Dogs don't understand what we say. Or so some people believe. It's true that dogs don't understand *everything* we say. But they understand a whole lot more than most people give them credit for. Great dog parents know that their dogs are listening, and they know dogs understand much of what they say. They also know that talking to their dogs contributes to their sense of security. Therefore, you must talk to your dog a lot.

Just a Little Information, Please

Talking to your dog helps her learn and get a sense of her place in day-to-day life. Imagine what it would be like if each day you woke up and didn't have a clue about what was going to happen to you. Someone else was running the show, and all you got to do was do what you were told. Some people may not have to work too hard to imagine this scenario. Maybe you have a job where you're told exactly what to do, and the instructions change every day. Or maybe you're in a marriage where your spouse cracks the whip and calls the shots. If so, you know what it feels like.

Most people, however, have some idea what to expect on any given day. For the most part, most of us are in control of our actions. (Though that claim is debatable on many levels, as well. I'll save that for another book.)

For example, when you wake up, you know whether or not you're going to take a walk that day. You know if you plan to work, if you plan to go someplace, if you plan to do chores, and so on. Admittedly, those plans can change because of things not in your control. (As author Carolyn Myss says, "If you want to make God laugh, tell Him your plans.") But for the most part, you have some idea of what you want to do with your day.

Your dog, on the other hand, has no clue what will happen when she wakes up in the morning. She can only hope for the best and get her cues from you. She watches. Are you putting on the right clothes to go for a walk? Are you dressing for a trip? Are you packing a bag for travel? Are you straightening up the house and looking out the window like you're expecting someone? Your dog watches, looking for hints about what is to happen.

Imagine the stress of this. You can relieve this stress by giving your dog lots of information.

"We're going to go for a walk," I tell Muggins as I head into the bathroom. She shakes and wags her tail, stretches, and whines a few times. "Mommy just has to get dressed," I tell her. This precipitates a loud sigh, another stretch, and a flop onto the floor. She's used to waiting for me to attend to my morning routine. When I finally leave the bedroom and head for the kitchen, she shakes and prances in a circle. "Now?" she's asking. "Mommy just has to take her vitamins first," I tell her. She plunks her butt down on the carpet and stares at me.

As the day goes on, you need to guide your dog from one activity to the next by talking to her. Your dog will listen and watch. Your dog will learn. Your dog's knowledge (which you provide to her through constant talking) helps her be more secure about her place in the world.

According to Patricia Gail Burnham, author of *Playtraining Your Dog*, "The more a dog is talked to, the more responsive it becomes to verbal control." I have certainly experienced this with Muggins. She is quite attentive to my words and amazingly responsive.

Jeffrey Moussaieff Masson, author of *Dogs Never Lie About Love*, says, "Expectation is essential to a dog's existence." Of course it is. It gives them security. Talking to them helps create these expectations.

From Counselor to Buddy

Why do you talk to other people? Because you enjoy the interaction, the give and take, the exchange of information and the emotional connection you get when you do. (Actually, emotional connection can be a rare thing when talking to other people, especially men, with the exception of Tim; but again, that's a whole other book.) You might think that there isn't much give and take when conversing with a dog, that there isn't much exchange of information. You'd be wrong.

Talking to your dog also can help you clarify your thoughts. Your dog won't respond verbally, of course. I can't say, for instance, "Muggins, I'm stuck with this column I'm working on. What am I going to do now?" and expect her to have an answer.

I usually do get a concerned response, though. I might say, "Muggins, I'm stuck, what should I do?" Muggins tilts her head, pricks up her ears, wags her tail, and noses my leg or whines and wiggles or licks my hand, or she shakes her body and runs to get a toy. She gives me *some* response. Whatever the response is, I feel like I've been heard. That's really all I want.

When you talk with someone, how often do you really want a response? Sometimes you do. But when you ask something like, "Should I wear the blue dress or the red dress?" you may not really want another person's opinion. In truth, don't you have an intuition about most everything you do?

Don't you just sometimes, or often, want reassurance about what you already know? Do you honestly not know whether to wear the blue or the red dress? You know. You just think you don't. So when you ask your dog and your dog yawns or wags her tail or jumps up and lies down on the red dress, spreading dog hair all over the fabric, don't you get an answer of sorts? "Trust your intuition," your dog is telling you.

And what if you're just shooting the breeze? "Sure is raining hard outside, isn't it?" If you were in Maine sitting on the boardwalk in front of the corner store, your buddy might say, "Ayup." Instead you're at home with your dog, and your dog bounces up from the sofa and runs to the door because she heard the word "outside." Now both you and your dog can watch the rain in some sort of mutual experience.

How to Get a Ph.D.O.G.

Some people think their dogs aren't very smart. We have friends who have a little dog that they constantly call dumb. I'll admit, the dog isn't very responsive to language, not the way Muggins and most other dogs I know are.

However, this little dog doesn't get much attention. The dog spends most of his time lying around, and most of the family doesn't interact with him much. How can the dog be expected to be smart if no one is teaching the dog?

Tim and I got to take care of this dog for a couple weeks while the family was on vacation, and during that two weeks, we spoke to the dog often. Just in that short amount of time, the dog became more responsive and began demonstrating a lot of behavior that was quite the opposite of "dumb." Clearly, the dog just needed some verbal interaction to develop his intelligence quota.

Do you want a smart dog? Start talking. You'll be astounded at how much your dog will learn. That's because dogs listen.

Muggins is a great listener. She's always listening to me, even when I'm not talking to her. She has quite a wide vocabulary. She has attached meaning to dozens of words, including but by no means limited to these: dinner, hungry, food, treat, turkey, outside, car, go, home, okay, stay, sit, down, roll over, off, high five, Daddy, Grandma, Grandpa, Mickey, Auntie Jan, Auntie Mary, Auntie Jackie, a visitor, better go see, insect, birdie, deer, horsie, squirrel, chipmunk, critter, kittycat, beddy-bye time, offsie downsie, get back, kisses, come, leave it, walk, beach, and do you want. I taught her some of these words on purpose, like "sit," "stay," "down," and so on. Many of them she just learned on her own.

Your dog can develop an amazing vocabulary if you talk to her as much as you possibly can. Give her constant verbal cues, and your dog will astound you.

That said, let me warn you that there are times when a dog's listening capabilities can be inconvenient. I can't say "beach," for example, without sending Muggins into a state of total ecstasy. She runs toward the back door in expectation of a jaunt to the ocean and whines until we get into the truck. I started spelling it out—B-E-A-C-H—with the result that Muggins has now learned those sounds as well. Now I say, "that sandy place by the ocean." I'm sure she'll learn that eventually, too.

You sometimes need to be creative when you talk around your dog. Most dog parents can't say "car" or "dinner." I've talked to many dog parents who spell a lot of words. And like me, they've discovered that their dogs soon catch on to the spellings too. When that happens, you have to come up with different words. That's okay. It helps build your dog's vocabulary even more.

It's fun having a smart dog. You get more quality interaction from the dog, and others enjoy your dog more as well.

How to Win Friends and Impress Strangers

Do you want your friends to love your dog as much as you do? It's easy to endear your pup to others. Simply teach your dog your friends' names and announce your friends' arrival.

A dear friend of mine died a few years ago after a long battle with cancer. Until her illness became too advanced for her to go out much, she would visit me weekly. Muggins loved her Auntie Mary. Before the time for Mary's visit, I'd say to Muggins, "Auntie Mary come see puppies." (Correct grammar isn't a necessity when you're conversing with dogs.) Muggins would jump around, whine, bark, and run to the front window to watch for the vehicle that would bring Auntie Mary to her door. When Mary rang the doorbell, Muggins would throw herself into greeting Mary with such enthusiasm that Mary was all smiles and laughter. She would say to me, "I know you think I come to see you. But it's really Muggins I'm here to see. I need my Muggins fix."

Of course she did. Who can resist the sweet, open love of an enthusiastic dog? Well, I'm sure some can. But those are people I don't really want to know.

Not all the people you know are dog people. It can be a strain to have people around who don't appreciate your dog or, worse, who don't like your dog. You can diminish these occurrences when you help your dog treat your friends like royalty.

Say What?

If you're not used to talking to your dog, you may not know exactly what to say. Here are just a few of the many ways you can converse with your dog.

Of course you want to tell your dog what you expect from her. The basic communication starts with instruction. Come. Sit. Stay. Let's go. Drop it. Bring it. These are like the ABCs when you're speaking to your dog.

But as a dog parent, you need to go well beyond the basics. Give your dog cues about what's coming next as you go through your day. Your dog listens to all the sounds that come out of your mouth, and she associates the sounds with actions. Over time, your dog will learn that when you say, "Do you want to go in the car?" you're going to get in your vehicle and go someplace. Your dog will know that when you say, "Let's go to the park," you're going to drive to the park and take a walk. You get the idea. You say something and then do something, and your dog learns to connect the words with the action.

Consistency is the key to this learning process. If you say something different every time you go in the car, for example, your dog will have a lot more trouble learning the words. However, if you remain even remotely consistent, your dog can relate the sounds to the event.

You can give your dog commentary on the day as well. For instance after vacuuming the house, I say to Muggins, "Whew, glad that chore is done. We hate vacuuming, don't we?" Muggins, who has spent the last half hour on the bed watching the noisy contraption with furrow-browed canine concern, shakes, jumps off the bed, and trots into the living room with her tail up. Yes, we do, she's telling me, and we're glad it's done. By talking to your dog in this way, you give your dog information that can help your dog feel better.

Your dog will begin to understand what is expected of her next when you talk to her consistently about what's coming. For instance, as I head toward my computer, I say to Muggins, "I need to get to work now." She sees me pull out my desk chair, and she drops to the floor and heaves a big sigh. "My feelings exactly," I tell her. She sighs again, groans, and rolls over on her side. She has come to understand that she needs to rest quietly while I'm working. Your dog can learn this way, too.

In addition to giving your dog instruction and information about what's coming next, you can also, of course, confide in your dog. Not only can this be very comforting for you, it's good for your dog as well. Your dog can sense the connection between you and your words. Even when your dog doesn't understand exactly what you're saying, the sound of your voice still gives your dog a sense of security.

One of my favorite things to tell Muggins is "I love you." I do it frequently. "I love you, Muggy," I say to her dozens of times a day. "So much," I say. "Loving puppies is the easiest thing in the world," I tell her.

And it's true. Loving dogs is like breathing. Easy, mindless. Only better.

If you want to be a great dog parent, you must talk to your dogs—a lot, every day, often, whenever you're with them, in the car, at home, or out in the park. Dog parents know that dogs are sentient beings with feelings and an amazing amount of intelligence. It is your duty and privilege to provide them with a secure environment in which they can optimize their intelligence, not to mention their happiness.

chapter 19
Not Isolating Your Dog

Dog owners can leave their dog in a kennel without batting an eye. Dog parents cannot.

"Dogs are social creatures," says pet behavior specialist Rod Cassidy. Dogs like company, not solitude. They are used to being in packs, either canine packs or human packs. They are not meant to be in cages.

In an essay titled "Mason the Dream Girl," published in *Dog People—Writers and Artists on Canine Companionship,* Cynthia Heimel writes, "I worked for various rescue kennels. The dogs there go slightly insane. Even with nice runs and good food and fresh water at all times, they're in prison; they hate it. They need to love somebody, preferably a couple of other dogs and a human. They need a sofa and a treat." Sure they do. They need security.

Close to You

Your dog wants to be close to you. As much as possible. Dogs hate to be left. They especially hate to be left alone. They really, truly hate to be left alone in a cage.

I left Dizzy in a kennel a couple of times. Both times, she came home dirty, angry, and obviously miserable, and both times I felt horribly guilty. I did this before I became a true dog parent.

Muggins has never seen the inside of a kennel. I hope she never will.

That said, I know not all kennels are created equal. Also, it's not always possible to leave your dog with a caretaker. Your responsibility is to make the best arrangements possible for your dog when you absolutely must leave her behind.

Let me take a minute here to mention crate training. While confining a dog to a cage, run, or crate all day is totally unacceptable, using a crate to train dogs and keep them safe can be a good idea. When Muggins was a puppy, I certainly couldn't leave her alone in the house, so I tried confining her to the utility room where I figured she could get into a minimal amount of trouble. She went crazy. She cried and peed and pawed at the door. So I put her in her crate, and she laid down quietly. Whenever I left her after that, I crated her.

A crate can be a safe place for your dog, your dog's den. You can use the crate to train your dog and keep her safe. This may be needed only for the first year or so of your dog's life. Usually, dogs don't need the crate after that. Some dog parents keep the crate around for their dogs' entire lives. As long as the crate is just part of the dog's life and it used to give her comfort and keep her safe, a crate is fine.

Thank Goodness for Family and Friends

One thing that can help you keep your dog out of kennels is surrounding yourself with dog people. People who love dogs, I've discovered, tend to flock together. We're drawn to each other, those of us who see the magic in soulful brown eyes and expressive ears.

I've been lucky when it comes to getting care for Muggins. My parents usually have been available to take care of her when I go out of town. If my parents can't do it, I have friends who will do it for me. And as I said, if I couldn't get friends or parents to care for her, I'd hire a pet sitter before I'd put her in a kennel. Generally, what Tim and I do is take Muggins with us, and if we can't do that and we can't find someone to care for Muggins, we change our plans.

Perhaps you're lucky enough to have family close by who can care for your dog when you need to be away. If not, you can cultivate relationships with other dog people and create resources for when you need to leave your dog behind. This isn't as self-serving as it sounds. If you enjoy the people you get to know and you enjoy their dogs, you will want to help them out when they need to travel. They'll want to help you out, too.

I don't choose my friends on the basis of whether they have a dog or whether they like dogs. But interestingly, most of my close friends do either have a dog or at least love dogs enough to be willing to have them around. One of my friends has a yellow Lab, Jake, who is such a gentlemanly fellow that you can't help but want to be around him. One evening when I was at my friend's house for dinner, she mentioned that she needed to take a trip and was going to have to kennel Jake. She was afraid he wouldn't eat while she was gone.

"I'll take him," I said.

That's what fellow dog people do. You know that kennels are not usually conducive to a happy dog, and you're willing to step in and prevent kenneling if at all possible.

The way to find dog-parenting friends is to talk to people with dogs. When you're out walking your dog and you meet a fellow dog-walker, strike up a conversation. This is how you make any kind of friend—you just start talking and see where the relationship goes. If you make an effort to talk to more people who have dogs, you'll have a better chance of establishing close relationships with people who love their dogs as much as you do. A lot of those people will be happy to take care of your dog when you're out of town.

Staying At the Ritz

If you don't have family and you haven't had any success making dog-parent friends, you're still in luck. Fortunately, most metropolitan areas have a new kind of kennel, a doggy motel. These boarding facilities often offer play areas where dogs can socialize, comfy cushions for dogs to sleep on, and special care. Dogs are played with, cuddled, and talked to. This is definitely an improvement over regular kennels. If dog parents have to leave their dog, this is the way to go. It's kind of like sending your kids to camp. You may be separated from your dog, but your dog will be having a great time.

To find a doggy motel, talk to the staff at your vet clinic. Most of them know what dog care places are available nearby. Of course, speak also to those dog-parent friends you're making. Search for the keywords "dog motel" online or in the Yellow Pages. You can also call the local humane society to see if it can direct you to a good overnight dog-care facility. Sometimes you can find overnight care for dogs in the Sunday classifieds of your local paper as well.

Once you find a possible doggy motel, check it out as you would a vet or groomer. Go to the facility and make sure it's clean and run by a friendly, knowledgeable staff. If other people are there dropping off or picking up dogs, ask them if they're happy with the service.

You'll also want to prepare your dog to be left in a social situation. Make sure your dog has been spayed or neutered to avoid pregnancy. Make sure vaccinations are up to date.

Many places will require an interview to see if your dog is properly socialized. Dogs who can't get along with other dogs can't be left in social situations like pet motels that allow the dogs to play together. You'll need to find a facility that keeps your dog separate if you have an antisocial dog. If you do have an antisocial dog, you might also consider getting some professional help to socialize your dog. You can find dog behaviorists in most cities. Or you can find them online and consult with them by phone. Your dog will be happier—and she won't have to be isolated—if you help her be a more sociable dog.

Lonely Hearts

Even if you don't kennel your dog, you can still isolate your dog to an unacceptable degree if you leave her alone for long periods of time. Remember, dogs are social creatures. They simply weren't designed to be left alone for hours on end.

Of course, if you have to work you have to leave your dog. But, again, creative dog parents can come up with ways to prevent their dogs from being alone for too long. You don't have to lock your dog up in your house for eight or ten or more hours a day.

In large cities and even in some smaller towns, doggy day care is now available. These great establishments are run by people who understand that dogs are not meant to spend hours alone. The service they provide is invaluable. Not only doesn't your dog have to spend hours alone, you have the added bonus of coming home to a socialized and exercised dog, one that will not drive you crazy the minute you walk in the door at the end of the day. You can find doggy day care in the same way you find a good doggy motel.

If you can't afford or can't find a doggy day care, you might be able to use a pet sitter. For a nominal fee, a pet sitter will come to your home and walk your dog, play with her, and feed her as many times a day as you would like.

To find a good pet sitter, again, ask your dog-parent friends or ask your vet or groomer. You can also often find pet sitters online, especially if you live in a populous area. Web sites such as *www.pet-sitters.biz* allow you to post a "pet sitter needed" ad.

To keep your dog from spending long hours alone, you can also, again, cooperate with friends. If someone you know is home during the day while you're gone, see whether you can arrange to leave your dog with your friend, and arrange to reciprocate when possible.

Isolation creates insecurity in dogs. When you can prevent isolation, you provide security. You also get the satisfaction of knowing you're giving your dogs a great life, one that's full and rich. That's the joyful job of a great dog parent.

chapter 20

Giving Your Dog the Safe Freedom to Be a Dog

They say good fences make for good neighbors. This may be true. I don't know. I do know, though, that good fences make for good dog parents.

Dogs need fences. Although they love to run free, dogs must be contained for their own safety. They need to have a place they can play without worry of encountering a car and without bothering others. Tying them up and leaving them alone is both dangerous and neglectful.

Could Someone Please Untie Me?

Tying up a dog for long periods is not advisable. Desmond Morris, author of *Dogwatching*, says, "The worst mental punishment a dog can be given is to be kept alone in a tightly confined space where nothing varied." A dog tied up, in my opinion, is tightly confined.

The law doesn't agree with me. There are no places I know of in this country where a person can get even a ten-cent ticket for tying up a dog. As long as the dog has food, water, and some shelter, it's considered okay.

But the law isn't what should determine how you treat your dogs. Your responsibility as a dog parent requires you to live by a higher set of standards. Those standards are based on love.

Love doesn't tie up a being you care about. Love doesn't stick a dog outside, anchor her to a chain or rope, and walk away.

Tying up dogs is dangerous. First, when a dog is tied up and left alone, she can be stolen. Second, the dog can get herself in a situation where she's choked.

The other problem with tying up dogs is that they will do just about anything to get free. This can get them in trouble. When I had Dizzy, Brad and I once left her in the care of Brad's brother. At the time, we lived in an apartment, and we had to be outside with Dizzy when she was out. We told Brad's brother that when she needed to go out, he had to go out with her, watch her, and then bring her back in. He didn't listen.

Being lazy and not caring what we wanted, he tied Dizzy to her leash and anchored the leash outside. He then sat down to watch a ballgame. In less than an hour, Dizzy, frustrated and probably outraged at treatment she'd never experienced before, chewed through the leash, got free, and then chewed and clawed her way through the screen door to get back inside.

My ex-brother-in-law's laziness ended up costing us a lot of money. And it took Dizzy days to forgive us for leaving her with such a dolt.

Please don't tie up your dog and leave her. If you're going to tie up your dog, you have to stay nearby and check on her frequently.

All About Fences

Before you get a dog, if you live in a house, your best move is to get a fence. If you can't afford a fence, ask yourself if you can really afford a dog.

You don't have to fence the whole of your yard. Depending on the size of your dog, you may be able to fence just a part of your yard and keep your dog happy.

The type of fence you choose will depend on the size of your dog as well. Chain link fences are stronger than board fences. Obviously, dogs that can jump high and big dogs need taller, six-foot fences. Dogs that dig need to have fences with chicken wire or netting at the base, tacked to the ground so it's difficult for them to dig out from under the fence.

You can keep fence costs down if you focus on functionality instead of aesthetics. Don't worry about having the prettiest fence in the neighborhood. What you want is the happiest dog.

If you have a very small dog, fencing can be as easy as putting stakes in the ground and connecting them to some chicken wire. If you have helpful, brawny friends, you can have your friends help you build the bigger fences. It's good exercise.

If you live in a subdivision that limits your fencing options, you can use an electronic fence. These fences are perfectly humane. An electronic barrier is placed around your yard, and your dog wears a collar that will give her a zap if she tries to get past the barrier. I've tested these collars on myself to see what that zap feels like. It doesn't feel good, mind you. But it's not painful. It's more annoying than anything else, something your dog wants to avoid. That's why your dog will stay inside the barrier. Talk to your vet about the electronic fencing option if you have any doubts.

If you're going to be a dog parent, you must be willing to do what's necessary to be a good dog parent. This means providing your dog with security and safety, and this in turn means not leaving your dog tied up. If you have no fence, you must be willing to spend time outside with your dog to get her the exercise she needs and keep her safe.

chapter 21

Having a Dog Door in Your Home

Dogs love freedom. Dogs love to be close to you. Essentially, dogs are conflicted about what they love. They want to be nearby, but they want to be given the space to explore and run. Actually, they aren't much different from humans. They want it all. Good dog parents know this, and in order to satisfy a dog's need for freedom, good dog parents have a dog door in their homes. A dog door is more than a door. It's a gateway—a gateway to security.

Busy, Busy, Busy

Dogs want to be able to tour their (fenced) yard whenever the mood strikes them—when they get an urge to check and see if the robins have left a fragrant bird trail across the grass, or if the squirrels have left an antagonizing scent at the base of that fir tree out back, or if the moles have made another intriguing mound in the flower beds. Dogs have things to do, routine checks to carry out. Dogs are busy, busy, busy.

Sure, dogs also want to go outside to pee and poop, but that's not what being in the (fenced) yard is all about. Being in the yard is about territory, and maintaining territory is an important job that requires diligent attention to detail. Meeting the demands of that job cannot be done in the few minutes it takes to "do their business" (translation: go potty).

An Eye on the Parents

Even though maintaining their territory requires time and effort, dogs don't want to be relegated to the yard for long periods of time. This keeps them away from their people, the other important job they have that requires diligent attention.

They need to keep an eye on you, know where you are, and be there to offer their love and support when you stub your toe or eat a meal. They need to offer their warm bodies for you to practice your stroking and petting techniques. They need to follow you around, lie nearby while you read a book, or press their noses under your hands when you're working at your computer. They have important jobs to attend to inside as well as outside.

The Grass Is Always Greener

So what's a dog to do? It's a dilemma, one that's usually solved with constant scratching on the back door. I want out. I want in. I want out. Ogden Nash said, "A door is what the dog is perpetually on the wrong side of." So true. Wherever they are, dogs want to be in the opposite place.

I am chagrined to admit that it took me awhile to figure out the solution to this problem. Most of the time I've lived with a dog, I've been a slave to this canine conflict. I've spent more time getting up and down out of chairs and opening and closing doors than I care to calculate.

Springers are pretty active, energetic dogs. Let's face it. When they're young, they're hyper. Sweet as the dickens. But hyper. Muggins was more conflicted than any dog I'd had. She wanted out when she was in. In when she was out. She'd follow me around inside and stop by the sliding glass door, stare mournfully outside, then listlessly pick up a toy and drop it by my feet. Her body was in. Her spirit was out.

I'd let her outside. She'd tear down the steps of the deck and race around the perimeter of the yard. She'd sniff around each tree and bush. When she was a puppy, she'd pause and dig a little in her ongoing efforts to excavate the sprinkler heads. Then she'd charge back up the steps and stand in front of the door looking in. Her ears drooped. Her tail hung still. She looked like a dog that was forced to be outside and never let inside. Her body was out. Her spirit was in.

I'd let her inside.

And so it would go. In. Out. In. Out.

Of course, if you do this let-the-dog-in, let-the-dog-out thing, you're still being a fine dog parent. The important thing here is that you're giving your dog what she wants or needs. But wouldn't you like to make it a little easier on yourself and make it better for your dog in the process?

Thank Heavens for Dog Doors

The solution to your in, out, in, out, dilemma is simple. Get a dog door.

When I got divorced and moved to a new town with Muggins, I had the opportunity to build a house. I remembered the in-and-out thing. I didn't relish the jack-in-the-box routine of up and down off the sofa to open and close the back door. For the first time in my life, I had a dog door installed in my home.

The back door is like most of my other lifetime back doors—sliding glass. So I had the dog door framed into the wall next to the door. It has a metal frame and a heavy, clear plastic flap weighted at the bottom with magnets that hold the flap in place. It has a metal door that slides in place over the plastic and locks when I want the dog door closed off and secured. The whole thing cost me about $100. With the exception of the money I spent getting my dogs in the first place, it's the best money I've ever spent.

Pet catalogs have a myriad of dog doors to choose from. Many dog doors can be framed right into the wall, in the same way I had mine done. If you're not handy, you'll need to hire someone to do this. Many dog doors, though, can be installed in a solid wood door, and some dog doors can even be used in conjunction with a sliding glass door. These are frames that fit the height of the door opening. You simply close the sliding glass door against the inserted frame. The dog door is at the bottom of the new frame. You can also buy slider screen doors that have dog doors built in.

When you buy a dog door, pay attention to the guidelines for determining what size door fits what size dog. Most dog doors list the sizes and weights of dogs that can fit through each size of door. The width of the door is more important than the height. A dog can duck down through a door that's too short. A door that's too narrow won't work.

This is good incentive for you to keep your dog's weight under control (an incentive beyond basic health, that is). If you get a door that fits your dog, and your dog puts on a lot of weight, you may end up with a door your dog can't use.

If you get a dog door when your dog is a puppy, be sure and get a door large enough for the largest size your puppy is likely to attain. Ask your vet how big that is. Most breeds come in certain predictable size ranges. You'll have more problems with a mixed breed, though, because sometimes it's tough to tell how big a mixed breed will get. Unless you're willing to upsize the door as the dog grows, it may be useful to wait until your mixed-breed dog is at her full height before you buy a dog door.

Gateway to Doggy Heaven

That door is the gateway to doggy heaven. Inside and out. No more conflict. Your dog has the best of both worlds.

You will find it's such a joy to watch your dog enjoy her freedom. When what you're doing in the house bores your dog, or when your dog decides it's time to check on the latest critter smells, your dog simply pushes her way through that door and goes out to her yard. When your dog decides she's done her appointed yard rounds to her satisfaction, she doesn't need to wait for you to let her in. She just comes inside, and she has the security of knowing that she can go back out any minute. At any time, she can change her mind. In. Out. In. Out.

It makes your dog feel important. You'll be able to tell once you have a dog door. Your dog will have that forced nonchalance about her, that "I'm cool but I'm pretending it's no big deal" expression that a lot of teenagers have. Dogs have it too. It's in the prick of the ears, the tilt of the head, the angle of the tail.

When Muggins is lying on the sofa with me in the winter in front of a warm gas fire and she gets overheated or bored, she simply slithers off the sofa and schleps over to her dog door. Whisk. Flop. She's outside. I look out through the glass and see her standing on the deck, her nose pointed up in the air, surveying the latest scents. Sometimes she trots off the porch to go explore the woods. Sometimes she lies down on the deck and stretches out to enjoy the cool air. From time to time, she raises her head and looks in at me to make sure I'm still where she left me. Then she drops her head down again. When she gets cold or lonely, she gets up and heads to the dog door. Whisk. Flop. She's back inside.

If she didn't have the dog door, she wouldn't feel free to lie down on the deck. She'd be too concerned about possibly missing something inside and afraid that she wouldn't be able to get back inside in time to get in on the fun. The dog door gives her a sense of security. She knows she can come in any time. That sense of freedom lets her relax into enjoying her outdoor time. When she's inside, she knows she can go outside any time. That sense of freedom lets her relax into her indoor time.

Good dog parents want their dogs to be happy and content and to have freedom and as much of a sense of control over their environment as possible. Sure, you'll love it that because of the dog door, you don't have to budge every time your dog wants to go outside. But more important, you'll love knowing that you have provided your dog with doggy contentment.

A dog door is a little thing, a simple thing. Yet it brings dogs so much pleasure. A dog door is an easy way for you to provide your dog with the security of freedom.

chapter 22

Giving Attention When Your Dog Wants It

Some dogs are willing to lie next to their people and wait patiently while their people work, read, talk on the phone, watch television, and so on. These dogs are content just being close. That's enough for them.

Not all dogs are this docile, though. Most dogs want activity. They want action.

Dog parents have no illusions about a dog's ability to lie still. You want dogs because you want to interact with them. I mean, why bother getting a dog if you don't want to have a relationship with one? You can get statues and knick-knacks for your décor. If you need home security, you can get an electronic security system. Dog parents want a dog for a friend and companion.

Goodbye Comes Way Too Soon

Dogs don't live nearly long enough. They're with you for such a short time, and sometimes that time is even shorter than what you're prepared to accept.

Dizzy was nine years old when she died. I'd hoped we'd get at least twelve years or so together. We didn't get it. When she was gone, I thought about all the times I could have paid more attention to her and didn't because I was too busy or preoccupied with something else.

You don't want to miss precious time with your dog. Your dog will be gone before you know it. You need to savor the dog-parent experience while you can.

Every moment you spend with your dog is precious. Every cuddle, every lick, every tail wag, every whine, and every minute of playtime is a blessing. If your dog wants your attention, she's offering you the gift of herself, and when you turn away from her, ignore her, or push her away, you're refusing that gift.

Attention, Please

After Dizzy died, I vowed I'd do better with my next dog. Which is a good thing. Muggins doesn't have the patience Dizzy had. When Muggins was a puppy, she nearly drove me crazy. She was a constant hands-on project. You didn't just let Muggins amuse herself and go about your business. She wanted your attention, and she wanted it all the time. If I needed to get something done that required my full concentration, I had to put her in her crate.

As she grew and matured, she got a bit better about being patient. For example, as I've said, she will now wait until I wake up in the morning before rousting me from bed. She will lie quietly nearby while I work. Still, her patience only lasts for so long, and then she wants my attention.

When I'm tempted to push her away, I think about Dizzy. One day, Muggins will be gone. I don't want to have the same regrets about her that I have about Dizzy.

You don't want regrets either. When your dog asks for your attention, if you can possibly give it, give it. Even a couple minutes of petting or playing can satisfy your dog, and it usually isn't going to disrupt your activity that much.

Hands-On Dog Care

You don't have to totally stop what you're doing to give your dog attention. For instance, you'll occasionally find me typing with one hand and playing tug-a-war with the other. I'm good at doing Pilates and giving ear scratches at the same time.

You can do this too. When you're working in the kitchen, stop every few minutes to throw a toy. When you're on the phone, pull your dog close and pet her.

My ex-mother-in-law is really good at rubbing her dog's belly with her foot while she does chores around the house. My friend Dianna can carry on a great conversation with me while regularly tossing the ball up in the air for her yellow Lab to catch. My dad can fix just about anything with his cocker spaniel, Mickey, nearby watching and waiting for the occasional word or touch.

My friend's basset hound, Casey, used to attack my friend's feet whenever my friend tried to talk on the phone. You could hear playful growling in the background and the occasional "Woof." Our conversations were punctuated with "Casey, no. Stop that. Casey, no." It was never said in a serious tone, so Casey, who probably thought his given name was "Casey No," didn't stop. It was part of the game. It never bothered me. Nor did it bother my friend.

Treat your dog like you would a person in your company. It's rude to ignore people. It's rude to ignore dogs, too.

Still the Boss

Dog books tell you that you need to establish who's the boss in a relationship with a dog. Dog experts are big on this boss thing. When a friend of mine was having aggression problems with an adult dog she'd adopted, she consulted with a professional dog trainer.

Her dog, a seven-year-old shih tzu mix, was growling and nipping at my friend if she tried to do something the dog didn't want. The dog trainer told my friend that she had to give the dog less attention; she had to ignore the dog more. The idea was to teach the dog who was boss and let the dog know that she wasn't going to get everything she wanted. The dog was pushing the envelope with her aggressive actions because she could.

My friend ignored the advice. She continued to lavish love and attention on her new dog.

Of course, my friend didn't reward the aggressive behavior. When her dog behaved aggressively, my friend stopped the behavior and corrected her dog. All the other times, though, my friend made sure her dog got a lot of attention. Eventually, the dog, probably at first nervous about her strange surroundings, began to settle down and respond to my friend's attentions by becoming a loving and gentle lapdog.

There's Pushy, Then There's Too Pushy

Of course, giving your dog attention can get out of hand if the dog is constantly pushing between you and other people. However, it's possible to balance a dog's needs, your own needs, and the needs of the other people in your life.

As a dog parent, you can make time for these things. When your dog dies, you want no regrets. You don't want to linger over the lost time, the lost opportunities. You want to celebrate your dog's life in all its rich fullness and know that you gave her the best you possibly could. This gives her security. It gives you peace of mind.

Let your dog know when pushing becomes too pushing. Make sure your dog understands what is ac able and what isn't. You do this by allowing the beha that's okay and either ignoring or correcting the beha that isn't okay.

For example, if you're okay with your dog bringing to to you while you're doing other things, by all means thro the toy. If you want your dog to bring the toy only whei you're watching television but not doing chores, only throw the toy when you're watching television. Dogs are smart. They'll learn what you want when you make your wants consistently known.

It's helpful to teach your dog some kind of "Stop" command. It doesn't have to be that particular word. But you want something more than just the word "no." You're teaching your dog that what she's doing isn't okay.

There are various ways to train such a command. It's a good idea to get a book on dog training—you can find dozens online and in bookstores. I've found it useful to teach Muggins that "Stop" means to cease and desist from what she's doing. Say she's pawing at my leg while I work. I take her paw and put it on the floor and say, "Stop." After only a couple of repetitions, she starts to get the idea.

Dogs ask for so little. When your dog wants your attention, she doesn't require your full and undivided attention every time. A pat, a snuggle, a toy toss—just an acknowledgment that she's there and she matters. It helps her feel secure about her place in your life. Surprisingly little amounts of time are enough to satisfy a dog. If you get up and play with your dog for just a few minutes, she'll be happy. When your dog comes to tell you that she saw something outside, all your dog wants is for you to get up, follow her to the window, and say, "Oh what a good watch dog you are."

chapter 23

Including Your Dog in Most Activities

As I've said, dogs want to be close to you. They want to be a part of your life. They like to be in the middle of things. They love to "help." Dog parents know this. Accordingly, they include their dogs in as much of their lives as possible.

I have found that almost anything is more fun if you include your dog in the process. Even if your dog is just watching––and let's face it, that's often all they can really do––having your dog nearby while you work or play is a lot of fun.

A Little Shadow

When you're home, your dog is probably almost always with you. Most dogs will follow you from room to room. Muggins certainly does.

When I am in the exercise room working out, Muggins lies on a dog bed that I put in front of the window so she has a soft place to lie down while she waits for me. When I'm in the shower, Muggins lies on the mat outside the shower door. When I'm in my office working, either she lies on the loveseat and watches the birds outside the window or she lies at my feet. Sometimes she gets fed up with waiting and she flips my hand up and off the computer keyboard. Sometimes I type one-handed while I scratch her behind the ears. It's not very efficient, and it doesn't speed up my work, but it sure breaks up the monotony and makes it more fun.

When I do some sort of household repair project, Muggins is right there, watching, sometimes pushing her nose between me and what I'm working on. When I clean the house, even though she doesn't enjoy the process, she stays nearby, watching. And outdoor projects are her glory.

It's More Fun with a Dog Along

In order to walk the edge of the yard inside the fence, I have to climb up a bank, hanging onto the fence for balance, and work my way past a thicket of salal. Muggins dashes ahead of me, crashing through the underbrush. I catch a glimpse of her fanning tail. She looks over her shoulder at me—are you coming? I check the fence for damage, a dull task. But by the time I'm finished, I'm laughing. Because of Muggins. She's made the chore fun with her eager antics.

Include your dog in your household and yard activities. You'll find that you'll laugh more. You'll enjoy yourself more. And you'll have a happier dog.

It's All About Bonding

Including your dog in all areas of your life enhances your interaction with your dog. It enriches your dog's life and gives her multiple types of stimulation. It also provides her with a sense of security, the security of being part of a team. Sharing the things you do bonds you and your dog and brings you closer together.

Dogs need to be a part of what's going on. They want to be involved in your life, not just hanging around on the periphery.

Dogs are meant to live as part of a pack. In the wild, the pack is other dogs. In our world, the pack is us. Dogs look to you for guidance, for love, and for security. Being with you as much as possible is the way for them to gain that guidance, love, and security. It is your duty as a dog parent to give your dog guidance and security. It is your *joy* as a dog parent to give your dog love.

Include your dog in your travel as much as possible. Include her when you visit friends (if it's okay with your hosts). Take your dog on errands as long as the weather and safety allow—don't leave your dog in a hot car or in a place where your dog is in danger of being stolen.

If you're taking a bubble bath, you can let your dog be part of the fun. You can leave the bathroom door open and invite your dog to sit nearby while you soak in fragrant bliss. You can enjoy the fun of watching tilted head and blinking eyes as your dog watches the bubbles form in the water.

If you're building something, you can let your dog sniff all the materials and then be willing to let your dog insinuate herself between you and what you're working on. You can let your dog see what you're doing.

Just Want to Help

Be patient when your dog wants to lie down in the middle of paperwork or rest her chin on the box you're trying to wrap. Your dog isn't trying to get in the way. She's trying to be close, and believe it or not, she's trying to help.

I love it when Muggins helps. She's especially helpful when it comes to wrapping gifts. She either lies on the gifts, the wrapping paper, the tissue paper, or the ribbon, or she sticks her head in the box as I put the gift in, getting wet nose marks on the tissue paper and depositing little surprises in the form of her dog hair. I've given many a gift with bonus white dog hairs included.

I've wrapped packages without Muggins's help, and I'll admit it goes a lot faster. It's not nearly as much fun, though.

Which brings me to sex.

I understand that many people lock their dog outside the room when they're making love. I don't like to lock Muggins out of rooms. Even for lovemaking. Luckily, Tim is a good sport. Muggins may not contribute to the passion, but she definitely provides humor when she attempts to join in the fun by bringing us toys or barking. She has a plush duck that she often brings us during our intimate moments. "Oh, it's the duck," one of us will say when she drops it on the bed. It makes us laugh. We also find it humorous when Muggins settles down to watch. You've got to be secure in your sexuality to allow a dog into the bedroom during lovemaking. I admit dogs can be a distraction, but their antics can bring you more fun than consternation.

Sometimes dogs can actually help with work. I once saw a television show about working dogs that featured a lab that had been trained to bring tools to people on a construction job. The owner said the dog had been unhappy waiting at home for him, so he brought the dog to the work site and gave him a job. The dog, tail wagging, climbed ladders and carried tools in a pack slung over his back. He was obviously one happy dog.

Allowing a dog to be a part of the action, whatever that action is, requires patience and acceptance. Dog parents have these qualities. Many dog owners do not.

No Need to Yell

If your dog likes to lie underfoot while you do things, you won't yell at her if you're a good dog parent. If you must move your dog because she's truly in the way, you give her a gentle nudge with foot or hand and say, "Scoot," or something similar. Muggins responds to "Scootch" or any variation thereof.

My ex-boyfriend, Michael, who loved to cook, was constantly bellowing at his dog to get out of the kitchen while he was cooking. You don't need to do that. You can let your dog be in the kitchen with you. Simply look before you step anywhere. Don't hold knives or hot food out over the floor. Keep them over the counter instead so if something is dropped, nothing will land on the dog. Talk to your dog and tell her what you're doing. Enjoy the little tail thumps that communicate your dogs' approval for your hard work and her appreciation at being included.

Including your dog in your activities can require a little extra work, some patience, and more time than you might have planned to spend. Sometimes, though, including your dog can help you out. Training your dog to do things to help you, or simply training her to be well behaved, makes your dog happy, too. Dogs love to please; they have fun learning. Whether you include your dog in your activities or train her, know that spending interactive time with your dog makes for a happy, secure dog. That's all that really matters.

chapter 24

Trusting What Your Dog Tells You

You've seen the scenes from *Lassie*, either the television show or the movie, where Lassie comes running in from the fields: "Bark, bark, bark."

The mother immediately understands that Lassie is telling her that Timmy is trapped and needs help. Smart woman. We could all learn something from Timmy's mother.

Now, Timmy's mother appeared to have superhuman canine-understanding abilities. She seemed to know *exactly* what Lassie was saying when Lassie barked. In real life, it's not that easy. But you can learn to understand a lot of what your dog has to tell you.

We humans like to think we're smarter than dogs. Good arguments can be made for this conclusion. I mean, we're the ones who figure out how to make a living and take care of the house and all that. Dogs, however, may understandably have a different opinion about who's smarter. Although a dog has the capacity to learn dozens or more words, thus gaining at least a working comprehension of our language and what we're trying to communicate, our ability to understand canine language is rather limited. Dogs must wonder why we aren't smart enough to pick up on their language, which by comparison to our own is rather rudimentary.

It's All About Cues

Even non-dog people can tell the difference between a friendly dog and an aggressive one—it's pretty easy to interpret threatening growls or wiggly tail wags. Good dog parents can do more than this. Dog parents are tuned into their dogs. You must be able to distinguish between play barks, there's-someone-at-the-door barks, and the deeper, more serious bark that says "Come here. Something's wrong." You learn to do this by listening to your dog and paying attention to what sound is associated with what situation.

The process is similar to the learning process the dog goes through to learn your language. You match up sounds with occurrences. How does your dog sound when he's barking at a squirrel or a cat? It's going to be different than the way your dog sounds when someone is at the door. Pay attention to the nuances of tone and volume. You'll begin to understand your dog better when you tune into the cues.

Good dog parents learn what the gentle paw tap on the forearm means, what a deep-throated chortle means, and what a high-pitched whine means. You learn the gestures and sounds your dog make, and you associate those with her desires. That way, you know when she's hungry, needs to go outside, or is just excited about what you're doing.

Ignore at Your Own Risk

Are you guilty of entirely ignoring some of your dog's attempts to communicate? I know I sometimes am. Even though I do try and pay attention to Muggins's cues, sometimes I simply assume that she's excited about something that doesn't concern me or that she wants something I'm not willing to give her at that moment, like more treats or more attention when I can't get away from what I'm doing.

It's not a good idea to make these assumptions. It's not a good idea to ignore your dog. When your dog communicates with you, she may be quite serious about something, and that something is probably something you need to know about.

A couple of years ago, for example, Muggins began lingering in the garage whenever we went out to the truck. She would sniff around, poking her head under shelves and around lawn equipment. Her tail wagged tentatively, and she whined softly. It was a concerned sort of whine. I'd have to urge her to come inside or get in the truck. I attempted to ignore her odd behavior at first, but then I started to pay attention. I began to think she was telling me that something, some *live* thing, was in the garage.

A week or so later, I discovered rodent droppings on one of the shelves. My suspicion was confirmed. Muggins had been trying to tell me we had rats. Her communication was clear—the sniffing, the concerned whine, and so on. It just took me awhile to catch on.

How frustrating it must have been for her trying all that time to tell me what was there. She must have wondered if I had any brains at all. She was making it clear enough for a four-year-old to figure out. Why didn't I get it?

Because I thought I was smarter than she was. I was wrong.

In her article for *USA Weekend*, Elizabeth Marshall Thomas tells the story of a dog who managed to press a programmed number for 911 and bark into the receiver when her person's breathing machine cut off. As Thomas notes, even though the dog was trained to help the person, "it was quite an achievement just the same." So it was. Good thing the 911 center listened to the dog's call for help.

You need to listen too. Your dog's information can at the very least help you, and at times it might even save you.

Just Call Me a Hero

You often hear stories about dogs saving their people from fires or intruders or the like. Dogs are good at warning their people about potential threats. Some dogs can even warn a person suffering from epilepsy when a seizure is coming.

One day, I was having a solo picnic at a state park. I was far back in an isolated section of the park. Muggins suddenly began barking. It was such a deep, ferocious bark, that I turned around to make sure it was really coming from her. Her hair was standing up along her back, and she made a rumbling sound deep in her throat.

I heard voices nearby, and soon a couple men appeared from a path behind me. They looked harmless enough—but Muggins was really letting them have it with both barrels. Continuing to bark and growl, she backed toward me and kept her focus on them. I stood and said something to them about her thinking it was her territory. They asked me an innocuous question and went on.

When I later told a friend of mine about this, I emphasized that I'd only heard Muggins sound that ferocious a couple times in her life—late at night when she was barking at some sound outside. My friend said, "Maybe Muggins knew something you didn't know. Maybe those men weren't harmless, and they moved on because of Muggins. If Muggins hadn't been there, you could have been in trouble."

I don't dismiss the possibility.

Learn to pay attention to your dog. Trust your dog. Your dog won't often bark, uh, cry wolf.

You're going to find that when your dog barks or whines at the front window and you go to look, there is usually a person walking by or a deer munching on a bush or a bird hopping along the walkway. You'll often be able to tell from the intensity of your dog's whines and barks what kind of critter is out there. When your dog sniffs around wildly, there has usually been something there worth sniffing. When your dog goes into a high-pitched excited, ears pricked, tail wagging bark/whine there's probably some critter actually present in the house or yard.

Learning to listen when your dog has something to tell you and trusting what your dog is communicating helps you. Listening, and heeding, your dog's communications warns you of trouble and tells you what's going on outside.

More important, it's also good for your dog. It makes her feel important. Your dog will know that if she needs something or needs to tell you something, you will listen and act accordingly. This gives your dog a sense of security. It makes your dog feel good.

Your dog's self-appointed job is to protect you. When you act on your dog's information and praise her for what she's told you, your dog will get all puffed up with canine pride. You'll know she's pleased with herself. You can tell. Because you listen to her. That's what good dog parents do—we listen to our dogs.

chapter 25

Considering Your Dog's Interests When You Make Life Choices

You love your dog, and you want to give your dog a great life. But what about your life? You have needs too, right? You have goals and dreams and desires.

Ideally, your dog will fit perfectly into your life choices. But sometimes that won't be possible. What do you do then?

As a dog parent, you must take your dog into consideration when you make life decisions. This might mean you'll need to give up something you want. Or maybe you won't. Being a dog parent may often require you to think outside the box to get what you want. You need to get creative about reconciling your wants with those of your dog's. What you don't need to do, though, is give up.

Walking Away Is Not Acceptable

I used to enjoy watching a television show called *The Good Life* on the Home and Garden channel. It was an interesting show that focused on people who followed their hearts and created the lives they desired.

One day, I was watching an episode about a couple who moved to Telluride, Colorado, to fulfill their dream of living in the mountains. They bought the perfect property and built their dream house. I was enjoying the story until the narrator shared this part of the saga: The couple had owned a couple of dogs when they were in California, dogs that the narrator said were "like children" to the couple because they didn't have children of their own. How sad, the narrator said, that the couple had to give up the dogs when they moved because the property they bought didn't allow fences. Because of this and the fact that the area was rich in wildlife, the subdivision also didn't allow dogs.

I was appalled. These people, though they may have claimed their dogs were like children to them, were not dog parents. Would a parent give up their child because the property they wanted to buy didn't allow children? Of course not. They weren't even particularly good dog owners.

A job or a relationship may move you from one place to another, but with a little ingenuity, you can always find a way to take your dog with you. If you make it a priority to have a dog-friendly home, you'll be able to find a place that will let you have your dog with you.

When you meet with a realtor, or when you talk to possible landlords, your first question needs to be whether dogs are allowed. Yes, you may need to pass up a really great house or apartment, but believe me, that house or apartment will never, ever give you the kind of joy and satisfaction that your dog will give you.

Besides, being a dog parent isn't just about the joy you get. It's about responsibility. When you take on a dog, you take on the responsibility that goes with that dog.

About the only time it's *impossible* to take your dog along is if you're ill and end up in a long-term care facility or if you're in the military and you get stationed overseas. Even so, when you're faced with this situation, you must still consider your dog. You must make sure you find a great home for the dog, a new dog parent who will give your beloved animal the care and nurturing she deserves.

Different Roads, Same Destination

Of course there's nothing wrong with wanting to go after your dreams, for instance, wanting to live in the mountains. But when these dreams negatively impact your dog, you may need to adjust them.

Let's say you're trying to improve yourself, and you want to get training in some kind of self-help or career area. You think you need to constantly travel to workshops or seminars. Maybe the only way to get the specific information you want is by going to a particular seminar, but that's often not the case. You can usually find the same information in books, on CD or tapes, or in online or teleconference distance learning. If you do need to travel to a workshop, you can always stay in a place that allows dogs and find a doggy day-care facility for your dog while you're in your sessions.

You think all this costs too much? Maybe it does cost more than it would if you didn't consider your dog, but remember your responsibility and your priorities. Every time you spend money, you make a choice. When you put your dog high on your priority list, which you need to do if you're a dog parent, you'll choose to spend money in ways that will be good for your dog.

So perhaps you have to have a smaller wardrobe in order to accommodate your dog while you travel. Maybe you need to take bag lunches instead of eating at expensive restaurants. You can go after your dream and include your dog if you're willing to make sacrifices in less important areas of your life.

And what about fun? What if you like to go to concerts? What if your hobby is hang-gliding or jumping out of airplanes? It's tough to include your dog in these activities. Again, prioritize. You can do these things from time to time if you balance these activities with a lot of quality play and bonding time with your dog.

Resent Me Not

When you love your dog like you love a child, you're unlikely to feel resentment when you give up something in order to accommodate your dog. But what if you do feel the occasional resentment? How do you deal with it if you're angry that you gave up a dream or desire because of your dog?

Your instinct might be to pull away from your dog when you feel resentment. But that's the exact wrong thing to do. You need to spend more time interacting with your dog. When you immerse yourself in activities with your dog, you'll be reminded of why you put her first. You'll reconnect with the joy that being a great dog parent brings you.

And remember, your dog isn't going to live forever (unfortunately). Maybe you're not giving up a dream so much as just delaying it.

I, for example, would love to go to Ireland. Right now, that's out of the question because Muggins is getting along in years, and leaving her for a couple weeks could actually endanger her health. Do I resent that? No way. I know that someday I will go to Ireland, after she's gone. Getting something you desire can even offset the pain of losing your beloved dog.

Besides, you may not always know what's best for you. What you think you want may not be what you need.

Dogs Can Make Good Planners, by Accident

Sometimes adjusting your life choices around your dog leads you to better life choices. Your dog may help you get out of situations that aren't good for you.

When I dated Michael, the relationship had a lot of problems, but one of the biggest problems had to do with Muggins. Michael didn't like Muggins. He thought she whined too much and was too spoiled. He pushed her out of his way. His dog was constantly trying to hump her or was bowling her over in his exuberance. Muggins was miserable. I wasn't much happier. I think I would have put up with Michael longer, though, if it hadn't been for the fact that my dog was unhappy. I owe Muggins a thank you. She got me out of a bad relationship.

Dogs don't have a say in what you do in your lives. They are forced to come along for the ride no matter what. This makes for a pretty insecure life. Of course, dogs are trusting, and they assume you will take care of them. To do otherwise is to betray the purest love you can ever hope to find. If you want to be able to live with yourself and your decisions, if you want to be a dog parent with integrity, you must consider your dog before you change your life in any way. Doing so gives your dog the security she needs.

Mountains or no mountains, no dream is worth sacrificing your dog.

PART IV: LOVE

If you give your dogs nothing else, you must give them love. As I've covered, fun, comfort, and security are necessary for an outrageously happy dog, but none of these are as important as love. Love is essential. Dog parents don't need to be told to love their dogs. Love isn't something you learn. The ways you express that love, though, can make the difference between being a dog owner and a dog parent.

As a dog parent, for example, you watch your dog sleep. You bury your face in her fur and inhale her scent. You let her lick your face. You talk about her incessantly. You use baby talk when talking to your dog. You always greet her when you come home or even when she wakes up from a nap. You take a lot of pictures of your dog. You give gifts and send mail on her behalf. You appreciate your dog's ability to help keep you healthy.

You can love your dog. Or you can *love* your dog. A dog parent knows about *love*. It's what you do best.

chapter 26

Watching Your Dog Sleep

Mere dog owners would never understand the joy of watching their dogs sleep. An owner might glance at the dog while stepping over her when she's sprawled out on the floor. Dog parents, though, get joy from watching their dogs sleep—I mean really watching.

Dog parents know that studying their dogs connects them with the dog and deepens their love.

In *Pack of Two,* Caroline Knapp writes, "I am in love with the dog's belly, where the fur is fine and soft and tan . . . I seem to spend a great deal of time just staring at the dog, struck by how mysterious and beautiful she is to me." Renaldo Fischer would understand. He writes, in *The Shaman Bulldog: A Love Story,* "[M]ostly I just loved to study his wrinkled face, fascinated by this living work of art." Knapp and Fischer obviously are dog parents.

A Furry Masterpiece

As I've said, Muggins sleeps with my husband and me (as described in Chapter 17). Every night, she curls up with her head on the pillow next to mine. She's usually lying on her side, her face pressed against the pillow, one paw tucked up under her chin. She watches me for a few minutes to make sure I am indeed settling in for the night. Then she closes her eyes, makes a few jowl-smacking noises, groans, and sighs. This is the start of something great.

I leave the light on and curl up so I can see her. I get comfortable, burrowing under the warm covers, and then I stare at Muggins's face. Her ears are relaxed, but the curls on her ears coil up in springy readiness. Her nose is wet and black. One pink nostril peeks out at me. Her eyes are closed tight. Her jowls are loose, and they flop on the pillow. Her paws are curled tight as if she's holding them in little doggy fists like a child curling up his hands under his chin while sleeping. Her rib cage expands and contracts in regular rhythm. Her breath is warm against my face.

I look at her even closer now, and I see individual whiskers. One whisker on the right side of her face is bent back toward her eyes instead of forward like the other whiskers. The short hairs on the top of her muzzle become more sparse as they graduate toward her nose. The fur and whiskers on her jowls below her nose are darker than around the rest of her muzzle. They remind me of a fuzzy caterpillar.

The curls at the top of her right ear stand up, but the curls on her left ear lie flat. She looks like she's sprouted one horn—only a little devilish. The way her face presses into the pillow narrows the white blaze that sweeps from her white muzzle up between her eyes to end on top of her head. The fur shines.

I stare at her markings. She has one circular black patch on her left side about the size of a tennis ball. When her hair grows out, the circle elongates and the black hair sweeps over the surrounding white. Black saddle markings across her back and sides also feather into sleek white fur.

I reach out and touch that black fur, combing it with my fingers, making clearer demarcations between the white and the black. Muggins opens her eyes for an instant and sighs again. She's used to me playing with her fur this way. She tolerates it.

I stare at her pink belly feathered with long white fur. I watch the fullness of her belly rise and fall. I am struck by how vulnerable it is, how tender and exposed. I look at her stub of a tail, tucked against her rear end. The feathering of white hair at the tip lies against her back legs.

I study the pads of her feet, pink and surrounded by tufts of soft fur. On her back right foot, she has a black freckle, my favorite freckle. Unlike most springers, Muggins has very little ticking, or freckling, on her legs, chest, and face. She's mostly white with those large black saddles and just a few other markings on her shoulders and rear end. As she's gotten older, some faint black freckles have started appearing on her legs. The freckle on her back foot has been there since she was a puppy. I call her Freckle Foot. I take that soft, perfect paw in my hand and cradle it in my fingers and palm. I run my thumb over the freckle, the bravest freckle, the one that has been here in a sea of white from the very beginning of Muggins's life.

Deeper and Deeper in Love

This is watching your dog sleep. This detailed study of a dog I look at every day, a dog who to another's eyes is a cute, if ordinary, spaniel, intensifies my love for her. It reminds me of the joy and comfort she brings me. It reminds me of her tender, precious soul, how vulnerable it is and how much she depends on me to care for her and keep her safe.

It reminds me of the years she has yet to live and makes me want to do everything I can to provide the best life I can for her. It deepens my love for her.

Watching your dog sleep renews your commitment to keeping her safe and secure. When your dog is running around doing her thing during the day and you're doing your thing, you don't often have the time to celebrate her very existence and relish the joy of having her in your life. You have those moments, of course, but they're fleeting, limited by the pressures of daily life. This time you spend watching your dog sleep is deep and intense. It brings your dog into your soul and draws her further into your heart.

When you're filled with loving tenderness toward your dog, when you're fully aware of the wonder of her very being, you give her a better life. You're more patient. You're more inclined to stop what you're doing to play with her when she needs it (as described in Chapter 22). You're more responsive to your dog's immediate needs. You're more in the moment with your dog day to day. It makes you a better dog parent because when you take the time to connect with someone, it affects every second you spend with him or her.

Goodbye Grumpiness

When Muggins greets me in the morning, I'm half-asleep and mostly grumpy. I'm not a morning person. But she is, so I can still soften and enjoy the greeting. The heart connection I get from watching Muggins sleep, moves me out of any natural grumpiness and allows me to be present in even early-morning moments with Muggins.

Watching your dog sleep is a wonderful antidote to a bad mood. Whether you're in a morning bad mood or a later-in-the-day bad mood, if your dog is taking a snooze and you want to feel better, take a couple minutes to watch your dog sleep.

The connection you make with your dog each day connects the two of you in a way that makes it possible for you to know when your dog is happy or sad. You'll know when your dog is nervous or bored or unsure. You'll know when she's troubled, and often, if you tune in to your dog, you can figure out the source of her trouble. The time you spend watching your dog sleep helps you receive the cues that enable your dog to communicate with you.

Love and communication—good dog parents want to nurture these connections between themselves and their dogs. Anything that enhances the bond of tenderness between human and dog helps you love your dog better. You may watch her sleep simply because you're smitten with her. The bonus is that by doing so, you're being a great dog parent.

chapter 27

Burying Your Nose
in Your Dog's Fur

I f you haven't done so many times already call your dog to you right now and bury your nose in her fur. Bury your nose deep into her neck or back or ears and inhale deeply. There, smell it? That musky, unmistakable doggy smell? Breathe in again. There's nothing else like it on this earth.

Food and Distant Places

Check to see if your dog's paws are clean and not caked in mud or some other unmentionable substance. If they pass inspection, put your nose to the pads of your dog's paws and inhale. Smell that? Fritos. Or tortilla chips. Dog's paws smell like corn chips. Go figure.

You might find that there are smells on your dog that transport you someplace else. Sometimes when you sniff your dog's paws, you'll be transported to the backyard lawn, so fresh and sharp is the scent that the green seems to linger on the tips of the fur between your dog's pads. Sometimes, you'll smell the sea. Grains of sand nestled between your dog's pads can carry a hint of the ocean—salt and brine, fish, seaweed, and seashells. Maybe you'll smell the city—that pungent hint of exhaust and asphalt. Overlaying the smells of these places you'll always notice the smell of corn chips. Earthy and rich.

It isn't just your dog's paws that are so compelling. The smell of a dog's fur is just as sweet. It's a smell that cannot be accurately described.

Dogs smell of doing. They carry their active lives in their body—the running and playing in wide-open fields, the serious trotting from window to door to guard the premises, the jumping around and over logs on a beach. This movement is recorded in their bodies; the recording leaves a distinctive scent, the scent of life.

Get the Connection

When you regularly bury your nose in your dog's fur or paws, you'll find that the scents you discover will be comforting to you. When you indulge in inhaling the scent of a dog's paw, you're celebrating. You're celebrating your connection with the canine mystery, the canine allure.

If they could bottle this stuff, it would be great. Instead, just keep a dog around at all times and occasionally lift up a compact, precious little foot and bury your nose in between the pads.

Perhaps it's the combination of scent and touch that makes the experience of smelling a dog's fur so enjoyable. As your nose inhales that scent of joyful activity, thick fur or the tickling ends of whiskers also caress you.

Your dog will feel the love. That love will foster closeness. You'll enhance your bond with your dog every time you inhale your dog's scent.

Eau de Dog

To my amazement, many people, either non-dog people or mere dog owners, seem to find dog smell offensive. I don't know how many people I've heard say, "Ew, wet dog!" as they wrinkle up their noses in disgust. I think wet dog is yet another wonderful variation of the doggy smell—a smell, in my humble opinion, that is only enhanced by the clean scent of water (or even the fishy smell of water). There's wet dog. Then there's wet dog.

After a bath, Muggins smells sweet—an artificial sweetness from the soap and conditioner. Pleasant, but not adventuresome. After a swim in the ocean, she smells salty and sometimes a little fishy. After a swim in the river or a lake, she smells of minerals and algae. All of these wet smells (with the exception of the bath smell) have one thing in common—fun. When Muggins is a wet dog, she smells like fun.

Muggins likes to stand in the rain. She goes out on the deck in a rainstorm and just stands in the downpour, her nose up in the air in pure enjoyment. When she comes in, she brings that fresh rain smell into the house with her. The rain smell then merges with her own canine-having-fun scent and becomes something even better. Wet dog. What a great scent.

Your dog has this great scent too. Enjoy it. Savor it.

The best way to enjoy your dog's smell is to keep her clean and well groomed (as described in Chapter 15). When you take good care of your dog, you can use your sense of smell to love your dog.

Dr. Nose

You can also use your sense of smell to care for your dog. In traditional Chinese medicine, smells are used to tell health status and to detect illness. Muggins has a different smell when her inflammatory bowel condition flares up. Having scent as advance warning helps me take action quickly to deal with the problem before it gets too bad.

If you're aware of your dog's normal smell, you can tell when something is wrong. The simple act of giving your dog an occasional sniff can help you help your dog.

It can help you keep track of your dog's activities, too. A little sniff will tell you where your dog has been. Muggins has a certain smell when she's spent a lot of time in the woods in our yard. I know when she's been sniffing around an old, rotted out stump (where I think a couple of opossums live) because she comes back inside smelling like sawdust.

A sniff will also tell you what your dog's been eating. Sometimes this isn't as pleasant as the other aspects of smelling your dog. If your dog has been eating poop, which dogs unfortunately sometimes do, you're not going to enjoy the discovery. But knowing it could help you keep your dog well. When your dog eats something bad for her, you'll want to keep a closer eye on her to make sure she doesn't develop signs of a stomach upset.

Using your nose is a good early detection system for potential canine problems of many kinds. It may be unorthodox, but it works.

Open minds are doorways to new experiences. New experiences take you outside of yourself. If you can move outside of yourself for a little while everyday, you can connect with some amazing sources of love in this world. One of the best sources of love I know of is dogs.

Dogs that belong to great dog parents are pure joy. They act it. They display it in their sweet faces and eager, wiggling bodies. They also carry the fragrance of it on their fur and in the nooks and crannies of their paws. If you want to inhale the fragrance of life, the fragrance of unconditional love and joy, smell your dog.

chapter 28

Letting Your Dog Lick Your Face

Dog owners tend to be squeamish about canine kisses. Never mind that humans kiss each other all the time, and even the most chaste of kisses requires personal contact— lips touching skin. Romantic kisses, all slobbery and wet, involve lots of tongue and spit. These don't seem to turn people off. Children's kisses tend to be quite messy, often including smeared food in addition to saliva. Still, almost everyone kisses, and we don't think a thing about it.

If you're going to accept these unsanitary practices, why be squeamish about being "kissed" by a dog?

Ugh, Kissed By a Dog

Dog owners would make the obvious arguments against letting dogs lick you: Dogs like to chew on nasty things, such as sticks that have been God-knows-where and bones from dead animals. Dogs often like to eat various kinds of excrement. Dogs lick their private parts.

But wait a minute. What about the things humans do? You touch all sorts of surfaces that have heaven-knows-what germs, and then you stick your fingers in your mouths. You pick up pens that other people have used, people who may or may not have washed their hands after they went to the bathroom, and you stick the pens in your mouth. Is this that much worse than what a dog has been doing? And as far as licking private parts goes, and forgive me for being indiscrete, many, if not most, humans enjoy something called oral sex. *We're* squeamish about private parts?

They say that a dog's mouth has significantly less bacteria than a human's. Canine behaviorist Ann Jackson has some objective proof of this. While studying microbiology, she was required to collect smears from the mouths of several mammal species, including dogs and humans. While the swabs from the dogs' mouths took three days to grow a bacteria culture, the swab from the humans' mouths showed growth in just twenty-four hours. Dr. Peter H. Gott wouldn't be surprised by these results. In an article published in the *North Shore News,* Gott writes, "You're probably exposed to more [bacteria] in a fast food restaurant than you would be from kissing your pet."

I can believe this. My dogs have been licking me for years, and I've never caught a thing from them. Yet when I spend only a few minutes around a human with a cold or flu, I'm on my way to being sick. Don't be afraid of dog germs. For the most part, they aren't going to hurt you.

A Lick Is Just a Kiss

Don't be afraid of canine kisses. In fact, encourage them. Allowing your dogs to kiss you communicates your love to them.

Dog behavior expert Stanley Coren, author of *How to Speak Dog,* says that dog licks aren't really kisses, as in expressions of affection. He says that we just interpret the licks as kisses. He claims that a dog licks for some specific, nonemotional reason—perhaps the dog wants to check out what we ate last or it likes the taste of our sweat. Coren says that a dog's licks often have a communication purpose. For instance, the dog may be trying to convince you that she's harmless and that you're the boss.

Well, he's the expert. I shouldn't argue with him. But I disagree that a dog's licks aren't *ever* expressions of love. Maybe they aren't *always* affectionate kisses. But sometimes they are.

Or at least I like to think so. And what's the harm in that?

Ben Williams said, "There is no psychiatrist in the world like a puppy licking your face." I agree. I love being kissed by a dog. I enjoy a warm, wet, rough tongue slurped across my face, bathing the palm of my hand or tickling the bottoms of my feet. When a dog licks you, the touch feels like affection. Yeah, maybe they're enjoying the smell of the chocolate chip cookie I just ate. Maybe my hands still retain the scent of the food I cooked earlier. Maybe they like the taste of sweaty feet that have been cooped up in socks and shoes all day.

If you watch a dog lick you, you see affection. It's in the softness of their eyes as they lick. It's in the eager prick of their ears.

When a Lick Isn't Welcome

Some dogs are shy about licking. When they are, often they've been discouraged by some confused soul who was afraid to be licked. These dogs might brush your hand with their tongue, once, lightly. They'll almost never lick your face. If you invite them to do so, they will give you one shy slurp with a look that says they expect to get in trouble at any moment.

Some dogs are enthusiastic about licking. Muggins is like that. From the first day I got her, she was passionate about thorough and forceful face licking. I never discouraged her. So she thinks it's her right to give people a good slurping.

She is well mannered, however, and will stop if a person indicates displeasure. She knows what "no" and "stop" mean. To make sure that your dog never enthusiastically licks anyone who isn't interested, all you have to do is teach the "stop" command. You should also make sure your dog responds when you say "no."

As I've said before, dogs are smart. They can discern one situation from another. If you allow kisses but another person doesn't, your dog will remember who is okay to lick and who isn't.

My parents, for instance, aren't as big into kisses as I am. Muggins knows this. After a couple initial attempts at kissing were rebuffed and scolded, she hasn't tried since. Your dog is smart enough to learn this way, too.

Dogs are also very good at picking up on nonverbal cues. A dog knows when its attentions are welcome and when they aren't. Most dogs will give up on people who aren't interested. (This is not the case with puppies, however, so you'll need to exercise a little control with younger dogs.)

No Such Thing As Too Much Love

Some dogs get really insistent about licking. Muggins is like that. At times, if you don't push her away, she will lick and lick and lick until you begin to feel like you're in danger of losing your lips or your nose.

Sometimes, she undertakes to lick the skin off my hands or feet. She loves to pin down with her paw the extremity she desires to bathe. Then she gets down to business. Lick, lick, lick, lick, lick. It goes on until I feel like the victim of a canine version of Chinese water torture.

Why would you want to let a dog do this?

Because it will make you feel loved. And because it communicates your love to your dog.

Yeah, I know all the stuff about what dogs are "really" doing when they lick, and I know about the germs. But when your dog is giving you kisses, you're sharing love.

Muggins looks inordinately pleased with herself when she is slathering someone with kisses. She tends to gravitate toward people who allow her to kiss them, as if she understands that she is being accepted when they let her kiss them.

I can relate to her feelings. I feel accepted by other dogs when they allow me to kiss them on the head or when they kiss me. Kisses bring people and dogs together. Letting your dog kiss your face enhances your loving connection with your dog.

Beauty Secrets Revealed

As a bonus, these kisses may also improve your complexion. For years, people have complemented me on my healthy, youthful-looking complexion. My secret? Dog spit. I think the daily face baths I get from Muggins contribute to my hydrated, clear skin. If I could figure out how to bottle dog spit, I would. I'd sell it as the newest rage in skin care. I'd probably become a millionaire.

Until I do, I'm rich anyway. So are you. You're rich in being a dog parent. You're rich in the affection for and from your dog.

You're rich in kisses.

chapter 29

Talking About Your Dog, a Lot

Parents talk about their children. Grandparents talk about their grandchildren. Egomaniacs talk about themselves. Dog parents talk about their dogs.

Talking about your dog is an important part of being a good dog mom or dad. If you want to celebrate your canine's life, you need to share it with people. You need to brag a little. Tell stories. People with any taste at all will enjoy them; I guarantee it. If a person doesn't like your dog stories, you may want to think seriously about whether you want to spend time with that person. You may be getting a glimpse of a serious character flaw.

Love on the Bad Dog Days

Talking about your dog strengthens your relationship with your dog. Talking about your dog helps you to be loving, even when you've been pushed to the limits of your patience.

Every once in awhile, you have one of those days when your dog is driving you crazy. Every dog parent has had one of those days. Your dog put her paw up to greet you and whacked you in the eye, leaving a scrape above your eyebrow—you're thankful you can still see. Your dog found a really special stick in the backyard and brought it in when you weren't looking, then proceeded to reduce it into minute splinters and leave it strewn all over the carpet. She spotted a squirrel out the front window and barked for five minutes while you were in the middle of an important phone conversation. This truly is one of those *dog days*.

On those days, even the best dog parents may not be feeling especially warm and fuzzy about their dogs. You get a little short-tempered and abrupt. After all, you are human despite being a bona fide dog parent. Even bona fide dog parents have their limits.

So there you are, about to reach those limits. At that moment, though, you run into someone or someone calls you, and the conversation turns to dogs. The other person tells a story about their dog, and the story reminds you of something your dog did. You tell a story about your dog. Suddenly, all the frustration that had built up washes away. All the annoyance is gone.

If your dog is nearby, you find yourself calling her to you. You stroke her head. You give her a kiss. Ah, the warm and fuzzies—they're back. All it took was a little reminder of why you love your dog so much. That's what talking about your dog does. It keeps you *in* love and *out* of annoyance. And if other people are having a frustrating day with their dogs, your dog story is going to remind them of their love for their dogs.

Spread the Love Around

Your dog stories help increase your love for your dog, but they do more than that. They encourage others to love your dog, too. In *Dog People—Writers and Artists on Canine*

Companionship, Cynthia Heimal writes, "My friend Patti always talked about her dog, Mason. Mason blah blah blah. Mason went to the beach, Mason blah, Mason has tapeworms, Mason doesn't have tapeworms, blah blah, Mason got her shots, blah." Heimal sounds like she's complaining. But wait. She then writes, "Naturally I fell in love with Mason sight unseen, especially since Patti's face took on this Mason-glow as she talked." Sure it did. Obviously Patti was a dog parent. Talking about her dog caused her friend to love the dog. So Mason received more love.

Talking about your dogs generates love.

A Story to Uplift Your Day

I'm always telling stories about Muggins and Dizzy. Dizzy has been gone for over nine years, but I still tell Dizzy stories. My friends love these stories. Or if they don't, they're clever enough to keep their feelings to themselves.

As much as I enjoy telling stories, I also love hearing stories about dogs. I could listen for hours to anything about dogs. I love hearing about their eating habits, favorite toys, idiosyncrasies, and favorite places to sleep. I even enjoy stories about dogs rolling in or eating something disgusting. If it's about a dog, I'm all ears.

Watch people's faces light up when they talk about their dogs. All the social anxiety disappears. All self-consciousness is gone. They're in the moment, sharing their passion— their passion for their dogs.

These discussions usually take place in the park or on the beach with the dogs in question cavorting around. But these conversations can happen anywhere, anytime. Talking about your dog is a great connector of people. It's a connector that can soothe frazzled nerves.

One year in late November, I was sprinting through a mall. I wasn't shopping in a leisurely manner. I was focused only on getting the items on my list. Vendors and shops were getting ready for the holidays, and the window displays were packed full of new merchandise. I wasn't interested. I wasn't interested, that is, until I reached a calendar store. As I started whipping past, my eyes scanned over the calendars, most of which displayed photos of dogs. There, on the second shelf from the top, was a springer spaniel calendar.

I made an abrupt left turn and charged into the shop. I went directly to the shelf, plucked the calendar off the stack and headed to the cash register. Total elapsed time from first glance to cash register—under ten seconds. When I set the calendar on the counter, the clerk said, "You sure knew what you wanted."

I laughed. Yes, I did. I have dog radar. More than that, now that I have Muggins, I have springer radar.

I pulled out my wallet and showed the clerk the only picture I kept there at the time. Yeah, you guessed it—it was a picture of Muggins. (Now I have a picture of Tim and Muggins together. Tim is smart enough to know how privileged he is to share the spotlight with Muggins.)

"You see why I want that calendar?" I asked.

The woman oohed and aahed appropriately at Muggins's beauty and asked her name. I told her and went on to say that Muggins was the greatest dog I'd ever had. Bless the woman's heart. She asked me why.

Well, like I said, I'd been in a hurry, but time stops when someone asks me about my dog. I proceeded to tell her how loving and sweet Muggins is and how smart she is, how she knows so many words and visual cues. Then the woman told me about her dog. She said it was a little dog, a mixed breed that seemed to have some terrier in it. She said it was the best watchdog she'd ever had.

We spent several minutes sharing dog stories. I left the shop smiling, not just because I'd found a great springer spaniel calendar but because I'd gotten to talk dogs for a few minutes. My whole mindset had shifted. Instead of being stressed and in a hurry, I felt uplifted and invigorated.

Talking about your dog will do that for you. If you're a real dog parent, you know this. You know that some of the best stories, the most heartwarming stories, the funniest stories, are dog stories. Forget kid stories or cat stories (though, to be fair, they're pretty darned heartwarming and funny too). Dog stories are the best.

You're doing the world a favor if you talk about your dog a lot. You're spreading joy and cheer. You're opening doors to shared experience. Really. Watch the barriers fall when you ask someone about his dog.

Bringing People Together

Asking someone about his dog is even better than asking about his children. People tend to worry about their children. Are they raising them well, are the kids adjusted well, are the kids learning fast enough, socializing correctly, playing the right sports, looking the right way––the worries go on and on. Though unconditional love is the ideal when it comes to raising children, it's a rare thing. The love, I believe, is unconditional, but the relationship is filled with expectations.

Dog relationships are much simpler, much more pure. You probably have only a few expectations of your dog. You hope she won't destroy things. You want her to do her bathroom duty outside. You want her to love you and be loyal to you. Of course, some dog *owners* do heap expectations on their dogs. They want them to be great in obedience training. They want them to show well in the show ring. They want them to be good in agility trials. But even most of these people are crazy about their dogs, and they love to talk about them. Their relationship with the dogs, their love for the dogs, is more important than how their dogs perform.

Just watch show-dog peoples' faces light up when you ask about their dogs. Breeders, too, are a blast to talk dog with. They'll tell you about their best lines and their pups and where their dogs have been placed. Again, there's a bit of the expectation, bragging aspect to their stories, but the passion and light are the same.

Dogs pull people from totally different lifestyles together. When you're talking dog, you don't care what the other person does for a living, where he went to school, whether he's married (unless you're single and the other person is as cute as his dog), or what religion he is. You only care about what he feels about his dog.

Anyone can talk dogs. Even the shyest people can tell stories about their dogs or listen to one of yours. Talking dogs is expansive. It brings you out of yourself, as so much about loving dogs does.

Don't be afraid to tell a dog story. People want to hear them. Really. At least most people do. Even if they aren't dog people and can't relate to getting excited because Rover's drool meets at a point under his chin, forming a perfect triangle when he's begging for steak, they can still relate to passion. All of us, if we're alive, has a passion, something we love as purely as dog parents love their dogs. You can open a door to let other people share their passions with you when you tell your dog stories.

Sometimes telling dog stories can be emotional cathar-sis, not just for the teller but for the listener. This often hap-pens when you tell someone about a beloved dog who was ill or who died. After Dizzy died, I talked often about her death. When I did, I almost always got an understanding response. Dog people would tell me of the death of their last dog, and often their eyes would moisten with the telling. Grief is universal. The pain of loss touches all of you and brings you together.

The joy of rediscovering a dog's love with a new dog, however, is even more binding. The delight of finding that a new dog can steal your heart just as completely as did the dog you lost is a commonality all dog lovers share. A few months before we met, Michael had lost his last dog, Nik, a four-year-old chocolate Lab, to cancer. Not long after Nik died, Michael got Buck, his yellow Lab. Even months after Nik's death, Michael still shed tears for Nik. The pain of Nik's illness was imbedded in the lines of Michael's face when he spoke of Nik. The joy of finding a new dog to share his life with, however, outshone the grief. I watched Michael connect with countless people talking about Nik's illness and his new love for Buck.

One day, Michael was talking to a man who had a choc-olate Lab. Michael told him about Nik's illness and death. The man told Michael that a friend of his had just lost his dog of a couple years as well and had written a tribute to the dog. He told Michael he'd have his friend send Michael a copy of the tribute by e-mail. This second man did send the tribute. But the man got the e-mail address wrong, and his note and tribute went to the "wrong" Michael, a man in a different state.

But wouldn't you know it? The tribute and note made its mark anyway. This second Michael was grieving the loss of a dog as well. The tribute touched him deeply. He wrote back to the sender, telling him that the tribute had gone to the wrong Michael but had helped him nonetheless. My friend, Michael, finally got a copy of the tribute by e-mail, along with copies of the note from the second Michael. He wrote back to both men, telling them of pet loss Web sites he'd found on the Internet. Three men, three strangers, were brought together by their common grief, by their love for their dogs.

The connection is out there. All you have to do to start the chain of love is talk about your dog. Dog parents know that the best topic of conversation in the world is dogs. Forget politics, sex, religion, or sports. Any of those topics can get you in trouble eventually. Talking dogs is safe. It's also fun. More important, it's a great way to love your dogs and inspire others to love their dogs and your dogs as well.

chapter 30

Baby Talk to Your Dog

Y ou know my baby well by now—Muggins, aka Pookie, Pumpkin, Sweetie, Sugar-tail, Snookums, Muggy, Precious, Sweetums, Princess, or Sweet Pea——Muggins and I communicate with each other regularly. We understand each other well. But ours is not communication of any great intellectual content. Muggins speaks in whines and wags, and I speak in baby talk.

Yes, I talk to Muggins like she's a baby, a toddler . . . a little sugar plum. I talk in a silly voice. I add "ie" to every-thing from "bird" (birdie) to "walk" (walkie) to "treats" (treatsie). My voice drips with honey. If you think this is odd, think again. Good dog parents naturally talk this way. You must be fluent in baby talk. Says Caroline Knapp in *Pack Of Two*, "I have about fifty different terms of endear-ment for [my dog] Lucille—sweet pea, and Miss Pea, and pea pod, and peanut, and Miss Peanut—and every once in a while, I'll hear myself in the house cooing at her in an over-enthused soprano, 'Oh, hello, you sweet, sweet pea! Are you the sweetest pea there ever was?' and I'll just pray my neighbors can't overhear me, I sound like such a goon."

Bridging the Canine-Human Gap

Although I suppose it does make dog parents look like fools to some uninformed people, baby talk facilitates good canine-human communication. Using baby talk is one of the ways your dog knows you're talking to her. Your dog listens to everything you say, remember? Still, your dog knows the words are just for her when you use baby talk. I believe baby talk is soothing to dogs. I have no scientific proof for this. In fact I have no proof, not even experiential proof.

So maybe it's not true. Maybe dogs are just as happy when you talk to them in adult-like tones in perfect sentences with precise syntax and grammar. Maybe they don't care either way. Maybe they just get used to however you talk to them—be it in pig latin, Swahili, or Klingon. I still think they prefer baby talk.

Talking to dogs in baby talk is a way of strengthening the special bond between humans and dogs. Roger Caras, author of *A Dog Is Listening,* knew about this method of human-canine bonding. He writes, "I make what I'm sure are idiotic sounds using goofy voices . . . They love it." Caras admits feeling silly about this. "It is a pretty good idea," he writes, "to be away from other people when you do it unless you want people talking and pointing."

I doubt, though, many people talk and point. Non-dog people may not understand baby talking to a dog. But they've more than likely used baby talk to talk to a baby. Why? Why is it most people revert to that high-pitched "cootchie cootchie coo" voice when speaking to a baby? Why do you stop doing it once the child can speak back to you? I don't know about you, but I don't baby talk toddlers. I speak to them in matter-of-fact words and tone. But babies, oh yeah, I fuss over babies, and so does most everyone else. I think human parents do it for the same reason dog parents do it with dogs. Babies don't understand a lot of the words you're saying. But they understand tone.

Similarly, dogs don't understand a lot of the words you're saying. But they do understand the feeling behind the words. They also understand tone.

If you don't believe me, try this experiment. Say to your dog, "You are a really bad dog. That's a NO," or something similar that generally has a negative effect on your dog. Say it in a high-pitched, baby talk tone. Say it in a sing-song voice. If your dog is like every other dog I know, chances are that she will wag her tail and look pleased. Most probably, she recognizes the words "bad dog" and "no," but the meaning is being negated by the tone of your voice. Your dog instinctively knows that the tone you're using is a loving tone that communicates that you're pleased with your dog.

Now say to your dog, "You are such a good dog. What a good dog." Only say it in a harsh, stern tone, low-pitched— whatever tone you normally use to scold your dog. Chances are, your dog will drop her ears and look hurt. She'll also look confused. She knows the words "good dog," but again, those familiar words are being negated by the tone you're using. Your dog responds more to tone than to words. Tone is something she can relate to. She can tell the difference between approval and anger just by listening to the tone of your voice.

Caras tells a story about his own dogs in *A Dog Is Listening* that shows how dogs respond to tone: "Duncan loves it when I insult him, while I am scratching him. 'You are nothing but a dog, just a dog, and I shouldn't be wasting my time on you.' His eyes get absolutely glassy when I say that, particularly when I sound like a poor imitation of

Mel Blanc." Obviously, Duncan doesn't care about Cara's words. Duncan hears the tone, which communicates love.

Think about it. Barking, whining, and other dog noises aren't about syntax. They're about tone. A loud, gruff bark is a "There's something out there" bark. A high-pitched bark is a "This is exciting" bark. Most dogs have a whole range of barks that communicate different things. Muggins has her "Come on, I'm bored; let's go" bark that she uses when I stop to talk to someone on the beach. She has her "I'm having fun" bark that she uses when we're playing. She has her "How could you have left me like that?" bark she uses to scold me when I get back from someplace after having left her at home.

I could go on, but you get the idea. Basically, the sound, the bark noise itself, is the same. What makes each bark unique is the tone, the pitch. That's how your dog communicates with you. It only makes sense that this is how she can best understand communication from you to her. So talk to her in baby talk.

Baby talk is a way to build a common ground for communication. Somewhere between barking and talking is baby talk. I think it's the compromise between human language and dog language. It uses the words we humans rely on to understand and communicate, but it also uses tone, which is what dogs understand the most. It is the best of both worlds. It brings human and canine closer together.

Baby Talk Is Fun

Okay, I guess I might as well confess the truth. Putting aside the important concept of bridging the human-canine gap, I enjoy talking baby talk to my dogs. Not just to my dogs, to any dogs. I have no compunction about embarrassing myself with a total stranger's dog. For some reason, baby talk is just plain fun.

Me: "Well aren't you just the cutest thing? You are, aren't you? You are a handsome boy. Just a pretty boy, you are. You want to give me kisses? T'ank oo for the kisses."

Stranger's dog: "Whine, whine," wag, wag, wag, "whine."

The dog and I understand each other, and I never hazard to glance up and see what the dog's human is doing while we carry on. I'm sure some people are happy to have their dogs fussed over. They might even see it as their dogs' due and recognize the universal dog baby talk language because they use it themselves. On the other hand, some misguided people probably think I've gone round the bend.

Then again, I've listened to a lot of dog parents talk to their dogs, and most tend to speak baby talk. You probably already know how much fun baby talk can be.

Real Men Speak Baby Talk

I've known a few men who think baby talk is only for women. They think it makes them less than a man if they use cutesy phrases and tones.

But it's not true. My dad, a real man if I've ever known one, a man who can build a house or a cabinet and who likes cars, trains, and guns as much as any other manly man, uses baby talk to talk with his cocker spaniel, Mickey. Tim, my husband, another manly man, baby talks to Muggins. Calling her "Pookie," he says, "Ooh, a pitter scratch," as he rubs her under her front legs. "My Pookums needs a little pitter scratch." His voice takes on a tone he uses just for her.

I've heard many men talk baby talk to their dogs—in parks, on the beach, in parking lots of malls. Tall men, short men, young men, old men—many men talk baby talk to dogs.

"Gonna give me kisses?" one of my close friends' husband says in a high-pitched voice to their black Lab. This is not a wimpy guy. This is a man's man—a big, strapping, white-haired, broad-shouldered lumberjack of a man with a full moustache, a normally deep voice, and a fondness for things like tools and heavy machinery.

Baby talk is not a women-only thing. It's a love thing. It's a celebration thing.

Dog parents know that sweetums wants 'em the very bestest of loves, and you want to give oodles of those loves as much as you possibly can, oh yes you do. Isn't that right, Sweet Pea?

chapter 31

Greeting Your Dog

I love the movie *Regarding Henry*. It's a great testimony to the joy that's possible when you simplify life, or when life gets simplified for you. It's something dog parents intrinsically understand. But it's amazing how completely the movie's characters fail as dog parents.

Hollywood Screw Ups

In a gesture that exemplifies how a serious injury makes him a better man, Harrison Ford's character buys his daughter a dog. She's been wanting a dog for a long time, and she's thrilled to get one. The dog is an adorable beagle pup that's lovable and eager to please. Then the daughter is sent off to boarding school. Henry is upset by this and in the final scene of the movie, he and his wife go to the school to get their daughter and take her home. The beagle goes along. When they get there, the dog trots up to the daughter and eagerly wags his tail. The daughter reaches down and pets him briefly, but her greeting is perfunctory.

The daughter leaves the school with her parents, and as they're all walking away, the dog jumps around at their feet. Neither parents nor child pay any attention to the dog. The happy family walks toward the camera. The dog is still leaping up at them trying to be included in the special moment. The last thing you see and remember about the movie is the dog being ignored.

That is, that's the kind of thing a dog parent remembers. Dog owners may fail to greet their dogs when they have been separated from them, but dog parents don't make that mistake. You know that a dog's greeting is one of the greatest joys of having a dog. As Michael J. Rosen writes in the introduction of *Dog People—Writers and Artists on Canine Companionship,* "being greeted each time [you've] been away . . . is a reminder that life is too unbearably short to feign indifference to any joy, however familiar and constant."

Your Grand Entrance

Writer Stephanie Miller knows the joy of canine greetings. In an article for the October 1996 issue of *Bugler,* "Mere Men No Match for Puppy Love," she writes, "Until I meet a man who does a ten-foot vertical leap when I walk through the door, I'm sticking with my dog. I mean, no man will ever look at me like that. You know, the look that says, 'Oh God, you're home! You're so great! You are the center of my universe! I love you!'" Miller has described it perfectly—this is how most dogs greet their people. At least, they will if they aren't discouraged from doing so.

Some dog owners actually train their dog to greet them sedately. I have no idea why anyone would do this. Why would you want to deprive yourself of the fun and frivolity of a dog's welcome-home greeting? Given that this is how your dog greets you, how could you not greet her similarly?

As dog parents, don't we have an obligation to give back at least as much as we get from our loving canines?

I sure think so. You simply cannot be a good dog parent unless you greet your dog profusely every time you come home . . . or come back in from taking out the trash . . . or get out of the bathroom when she's been waiting patiently right outside the door, when she wags her tail in relief that you didn't fall in the toilet . . . or when she wakes up from a nap.

Muggins likes me to hold her paws when we're greeting each other. She sits up on her back legs and sort of hugs me. I hold her paws and let her lick my face. She whines as she licks, which makes for some pretty amusing sounds. While she whines and licks, I talk to her.

Here's the proper response to your dog's greeting:

"Oh yes, I missed you too," you say in that baby-talk tone. "Did you have a good time while I was gone? You did?"

Whine, lick, whine, lick.

"What did you do?"

Whine, lick, whine, lick.

"I'm so glad you had a good time, baby girl. Oh yes, Snookums, I missed you so much."

An appropriate greeting for your dog depends on the level of enthusiasm your dog shows you and on how long you've been gone. But the important thing is to give as good as you get. Be willing to go overboard to give your dog an effusive greeting.

It Seems Like You Were Gone Forever

As I said, your dogs need to get these greetings *whenever* you've been separated, not just when you get home. Dogs want to be greeted even when they've been separated from you for a short period of time. Like when you step into the garage for a few minutes and leave them inside. Like when you run out to the street to get the mail. These greetings don't need to be so involved. A simple, "Hey Sweetums, miss me?"

Arrwoo woo.

"I missed you too."

Wooo arrwoo.

"Yes, you get a treat." (Refer to Chapter 16 for more information on the appropriate use of treats.)

Dogs like to be greeted when they wake up from a nap. Here's a possible greeting (in the appropriate baby talk):

"Did you wake up from your nappie?"

Wag.

"You did?"

Wag.

"Did you have a good nappie?"

Wag, wag. Lick.

"I'm so glad."

Hug your dog and kiss her on the top of her head. Your dog will wag her tail again and wander off, contented. All is well. The world is still the same since she went to sleep. Mommy or Daddy still loves her. Whatever doggy nightmares she might have had aren't real, and she is secure in her place and in your love for her.

Hello Means Love

That's what greeting a dog is about—love. The pureness of a dog's love for you is apparent in everything she does. This is most obvious in a dog's greeting. Would you ignore a child's greeting? Your spouse's? Your friend's? If you would, you need to work on being a warmer human being before you work on being a better dog parent.

It is not wise to ignore love—in whatever form it comes. A dog's love is one of the best forms there is. You need to embrace it. You also need to make sure you give it back. You need to give love to your dog at every opportunity. Every greeting is a chance to give that love. Don't miss any of those chances, even if you've been gone for less than a second.

Every "bark, bark, arrwoo" requires the appropriate response: I missed you too.

chapter 32

Taking Lots of Pictures of Your Dog

My new friend innocently says, "Sure," when I ask if she wants to see pictures of Muggins. I can only imagine what she's thinking when I haul out the four thick photo albums and plunk them on the coffee table. Is that an inward groan I hear?

Dog owners occasionally take pictures of their dogs. You might see the dog peaking out from behind the kids or lying nearby in a family group shot. Once in awhile, you get a solo shot of the dog doing something cute. If they were inclined to have a photo album exclusively for their dogs, dog owners would have a small album, perhaps half full.

Something to Remember Me By

Dog parents, on the other hand, have pictures coming out the kazoo. Even if you're not great at taking pictures and don't otherwise snap many photographs, you need to have tons of pictures of the dog. Your dog is always doing something cute.

As I've said, your dog won't be with you for nearly enough time. This is one of the reasons you need to take so many pictures. You'll want to capture as much of your dog's life as you can so you have those memories to cherish after your dog is gone. That's what dog parents do. We take pictures of our doggy children because we're building memory books to sustain us long after our babies are gone.

Through the Eyepiece of Love

When you take pictures of your dog, you're doing more than building memories. You're also loving your dog by taking so many pictures. When you're looking at your dog with an eye toward a photograph, you tend to see her a little more clearly. It's a bit like watching your dog sleep. The focus enhances your relationship by shining a loving spotlight on the dog.

Taking pictures also makes your dog feel loved. At least, that's my theory. If you take enough pictures of your dog, your dog actually will begin hamming it up for the camera. Dogs new to a camera tend to run over and sniff the camera when you get it out. Dogs who are used to being photographed, dogs like Muggins, for example, tend to pose.

Muggins is, if I may humbly say, extremely photogenic. She takes a beautiful picture. She seems to know this. The camera is her cue to assume some adorable position and look as stunning as possible. I swear she practices her poses in front of the mirror on the rare occasions when I'm not at home.

The dog owner who takes only the occasional picture find it difficult to capture that cute pose because when the owner gets out the camera, hoping to sneak up on the dog as she sleeps with her paw on top of the family cat's head, the dog spots the camera, thinks, "What's that?" and jumps up to investigate. Dog parents who take lots of pictures are more likely to be able to count on their dogs to glance at the camera and remain where they are. These dogs know they're being watched. They seem to know that they're doing something special enough for a bit of extra attention. They bask in that attention.

I believe that attention makes a dog feel loved. How could it not? Wouldn't you feel loved if someone were always snapping pictures of you? Dog experts are quick to tell you that dogs don't think or feel like humans and that attributing human reasoning and emotion to canines is a mistake. My observation of dogs suggests otherwise. Dogs have an uncanny way of acting and reacting exactly like humans. Is it such a leap to think that focusing a camera on them makes them feel like they're getting attention, thereby making them feel loved?

Point your camera at your dog as often as you can. It's an easy way to say, "I love you."

This Is My Best Side

When you take a lot of photos of your dog, you tend to share them. When you share them, other people become enamored of your dog, people who might not otherwise see your dog doing all the adorable things you take pictures of.

Muggins, for example, tends to be a bit hyper when other people are around. Only my parents and a few choice friends get to see the cuddly, huggable side of Muggins. Of course, she's still lovable even when she's running around like a furry black-and-white banshee. But it's a bit easier to "ooohhh" and "aaaahhh" over her when you see a picture of her snuggled up on a pile of pillows.

When you show pictures of your dog being cute to other people, they tend to soften toward your dog. People will treat your dog with even more love.

Remember Your Priorities

Then there are professional photos. You definitely want to have these done.

I have got a great studio shot of Muggins sitting up in her proud, "What's up?" sort of way. The picture sits on the entertainment center in my living room. Several years later, I took her to a studio again and got a couple of adorable portraits—one with her sitting in a bucket looking a bit bemused and one with pink overtones, her sprawling on a white fur rug looking every bit the princess she is. Guests never fail to comment on these pictures, which hang on the walls in my home. Professional photos will make you a better dog parent because they reflect the importance you place on your dog's role in your life.

Remember the priorities you need to establish when you're a dog parent and how you need to take your dog into consideration when you make life decisions? It's a lot easier to keep your priorities straight, and it's a lot easier to remember your responsibility, when you have a professional photo to remind you of how much you value your dog. Glancing at that photo regularly can also help dissipate any resentment that might come up because of sacrifices you make for your dog.

I could be making this picture-taking thing more complicated than it really is. The bottom line is that you'll want to take a lot of pictures of your dog because you're crazy about your dog and you think the dog is just so darned cute that you can't help yourself. That pride in your dog translates into love, love that your dog can feel, love that brings you even closer together with your dog. Great dog parents do whatever it takes, even if it includes investing hundreds of dollars in film and developing or investing in a digital camera and photo printer, to strengthen that love and solidify that bond.

chapter 33

Giving Gifts and Sending Mail on Behalf of Your Dog

Throughout the history of canine ownership, dog owners have used dogs. They have used them to herd farm animals, hunt for game, and to find people and lost things and illegal things. People have even used dogs to help fight wars.

Dogs don't seem to mind this. In fact, they like to work and enjoy feeling useful. A dog with a job is usually a happy dog, at least if she's well cared for.

Dogs don't usually get much in return for the way people use them. Maybe a pat on the head and a "Good dog." That's about it.

Dog parents, though they may at times use their dogs to help them with some aspect of their lives, do not use their dogs without making sure that the dog gets some benefit from the activity as well. Using your dogs to give gifts and cards is an example of how this works.

Gifts from Dogs Are Just More Fun

My dogs have been giving gifts and cards for years. On birthdays, Mother's Day and Father's Day, and Christmas, my dogs have always gotten my loved ones cards and/or gifts. Of course the dogs don't actually come up with the ideas for gifts, buy the gifts, wrap the gifts, and give the gifts. I'm the one doing all that. I'm using my dog as a front canine. I come up with the idea, buy the gift, wrap it, and sign the card . . . from my dog.

Sounds like the dog is getting all the credit, huh? So how does this use the dog?

It uses the dog to connect with other people and to delight people. I've discovered that people love getting gifts and cards from a dog. It's fun and amusing. For some reason, it also makes people feel even more special than if you had given them a gift from you yourself.

I know *I* love getting gifts from animals. It's as if the gift comes with an extra layer of caring. Of course, I know the gift actually comes from the dog's person, but it feels good that they thought to give me a gift in their dog's name. It's memorable.

It's Hard to Type with Paws

Since I got my computer, Muggins has been sending people e-mail greetings. Sometimes she just joins in with me, but sometimes she sends a solo greeting. She especially likes sending cards to other dogs. This particularly delights people.

I can understand it. I love it when I get e-mails from a dog. This is especially true if the dog attaches a self-photograph to the message. What could better brighten your day than a sweet electronic missive from a cute dog?

You're not going to be able to teach your dog to use a keyboard, but you can help her use your computer to make others happy. Write on your dog's behalf. Let your dog trot into cyberspace and delight your friends with cute messages.

Gifts, Gifts, Everywhere Gifts

Giving gifts in your dog's name is a good way to give little things, a way to do something a little extra for someone. You can give a gift from you, but you also can give the special person a little something from your dog, too.

Different dogs can give different gifts for different holidays. One of my friends has a couple of mischievous dogs that enjoy giving goodies for Halloween because that's the night when tricks are okay. Perhaps your German shepherd wants to give a gift for Veteran's Day. Or maybe your herding dog wants to give a gift for Labor Day. Muggins celebrates April Fool's Day, partly because it's my birthday as well, but partly because it's a fool's day, and "Muggins" means dupe or fool in Old English.

It would be appropriate for any dog to give a gift on Arbor Day. Dogs, especially male dogs, love trees. Dogs can celebrate their need for off-leash runs and the freedom that gives them by giving gifts for Independence Day. And of course, a dog that has great parents will want to celebrate Mother's Day and Father's Day.

If you have the time and inclination, you can really have a lot of fun with this. Do a little research on some more obscure special days. See if any match up with your dog's personality and then give a gift to celebrate the day. You can find a list of bizarre holidays online at *www.holidayinsights.com*. Dogs, for example, will get a kick out of Blame Somebody Else Day (April 13) and Go for a Ride Day (November 22).

A dog can even declare his or her very own day. Why not? Muggins, for instance, could give gifts because it's Muggins's Day. You can declare a day for your dog too.

Dizzy's birthday was June 5. After she died, I declared June 5 to be Dizzy Day, and every June 5, I plant a new shrub in my yard. Declaring a day for a dog you've loved and lost is a great way to memorialize your beloved dog.

Okay, so maybe your dog isn't going to enjoy this as much as you are. But what makes you happy makes you a better dog parent, and whatever makes you a better dog parent is good for your dog.

Getting to Know You

Letting your dog give a gift is an especially useful way to give a gift to someone you don't know well. You want to do something nice for someone, but you aren't sure if it's too much. If your dog does it, it's sure to bring a smile, and if you overstep some bound of etiquette, you'll be forgiven.

Giving cards from your dog can bring you closer together to people you don't know well. A few years ago, I met the couple who live down the street from me. I barely knew them and didn't have a lot in common with them, but I enjoyed their company when we met. They have an adorable dog. So after our visit, I sent them a note from Muggins. Actually, it was a note to Gizmo, the dog, from Muggins. Essentially, it was just a clever and different way to send a thank you for our visit.

You can really let your creativity loose when you give cards and gifts from your dog. Get yourself a dog-paw stamp that you can use to stamp cards with when you're giving them from your dog. Wrap the gifts from your dog in paper that has a dog theme. You can have the gifts your dog gives tie to dogs in general or to your dog's specific breed. Give some breed-specific stationary or a mug. Have your dog give food items that your dog loves (food items that people can eat too) or anything to do with the outdoors. Your dog can also give books, because, according to Muggins, people who read have time to pet a dog.

Any opportunity to make someone smile is an opportunity you need to grab. Giving in the name of your dog helps you grab some of those opportunities.

Here a Gift, Everywhere Love

Now, of course your dog really knows nothing about your practice of sending cards, gifts, and e-greetings in her name. Your dog couldn't care less. So you're using her. But your dog gets love in the bargain.

Giving gifts from your dog will make your dog a popular dog. Muggins, for instance, has several "aunties," her grandparents, and other friends who know she's a generous giver. Giving cards and gifts in your dog's name is good for your dog's image.

Do dogs care about their image? Probably not. However, a dog with a good image is one who will be treated well by everyone who knows her.

I have a friend who consistently sends me gifts from her dogs. She also sends Muggins gifts from her dogs. She also sends gifts from her cats and birds. This last Christmas, Muggins got six Christmas gifts from this friend—that is, from my friend's two dogs, two cats, and two birds. I haven't met these animals, but I'm predisposed to love them. My friend obviously is predisposed to love Muggins.

All this giving in your animals' names just paves the way for more love. More love is what parenting a dog is all about.

chapter 34

Allowing Your Dog to Help You Stay Healthy and Alive

One of the first things experts suggest that you teach your dog is to heel. Although I concede that this would be a convenient command for my dog to know, I've never found it indispensable. Heeling just isn't that important to me.

Healing, on the other hand, is essential.

Most people know that dogs provide companionship and, as an extension, comfort. Not everyone, however, is aware that dogs also have the capacity to heal.

A Guide Dog for Getting Out of a Dark Hole

I didn't discover how important a dog is for healing until I got Muggins. Before Muggins, I had the usual little health challenges—flus, colds, and stomach upsets. When I was lying in bed with a cold or flu, Dizzy was always there with me, often lying with her head on my foot, moving closer if my convalescence suddenly involved something to do with food. Her presence comforted me and helped me through my misery. It probably also helped me heal faster, but I didn't know that at the time.

A few months after I got Muggins, however, I faced my biggest health challenge—severe depression. I was diagnosed with manic depression, and I began receiving treatment that included over a dozen medications in various combinations prescribed for various lengths of time, all meant to try and control my debilitating spirals into depression. None of them helped much.

Enter Muggins. Muggins, still a puppy, was definitely a remedy for depression. It's difficult to spend your time lying around in despair when you've got a bright-eyed puppy dropping toys in your lap.

But my illness was more serious than a few blue days, and the depression side of a bipolar disorder deepened until I eventually became suicidal. By that time, Muggins was over a year old, and she and I had a loving bond. Even in my diminished state, I was her life, and she loved me devotedly and faithfully. She relied on me to play with her, cuddle her, take her on walks, and feed her.

One horrible day, despite Muggins's companionship, I had finally given in to the despair that depression created in my mind. Then Muggins nosed my hand. When my gaze fell on her adoring brown eyes and her eager, expectant expression, I knew I couldn't go through with my plan. The people in my life might be able to come to terms with what I was about to do; they might understand it intellectually even if they couldn't in their hearts. But Muggins—Muggins would never understand on any level. All she'd know is that I left her. I couldn't do that to her. I knew, even in my distorted mental state, that no one would be able to take care of Muggins as well as I could.

So I began a journey back to health. If I wasn't going to leave this life that felt so miserable because I was sick, then I needed to find a way to be well.

As if lifesaving isn't enough, your dog can help you find wellness too. Your dog will help because your dog will insist that you play and walk. Your dog simply won't let you stay in bed or skip jaunts in the park or on the beach. Your dog will make you walk. Together, you and your dog can walk your way to health.

Your dog knows you need to stick around, and your dog knows you need to move. Your dog also knows you need to laugh.

Need a Good Laugh?

Laughter is healing. In 1964, Norman Cousins was dying of what was diagnosed as a fatal connective-tissue disease. Cousins, determined to live, used laughter to heal his illness. He credits hours and hours of watching comedy with helping him survive. In 1979, he published *Anatomy of an Illness*, which describes his victory over disease using laughter as a weapon. Since then, many studies have linked laughter to improved health.

Laughter and joy can help your body recover from injury and beat illness. Dogs are one of the best sources of laughter and joy. At least Muggins is. I think she must have read Cousins's book. She seems to know exactly when she needs to clown to help me get through illness.

When I'm in bed, battling a bout of depression or other illness, Muggins brings me toys. Lots and lots of toys. Then she bounds around and attacks my feet or my hands and makes hilarious arrooing noises. Maybe she's just amusing herself. But her agenda also seems to be to get me to smile.

Let your dog make you laugh. Every chuckle and guffaw your dog elicits from you will enhance your health.

The Calming Canine Influence

When your dog isn't being crazy and making you laugh, your dog will be soothing you, simply by her presence. According to many studies, having a dog around helps lower blood pressure. Dogs are calming. When it comes to healing, a calm state is essential. Dogs are the key to a calm state.

I have a friend who went through chemotherapy in her battle with cancer. Her dog, Mayz, an active coonhound, was only a few months old when the ordeal began. Mayz played a huge role in helping my friend through her struggle. "I don't know how I'd have gotten through the days if it wasn't for Mayz," my friend told me.

When you're anxious, agitated, or tense, pet your dog. You'll make your dog happy because you'll be giving your dog attention, and you'll be doing something good for you too.

Lending a Helping Paw

Thousands of people rely on dogs to help them cope with serious illness or disability. A 1996 two-year study published in *The Journal of the American Medical Association* found that service dogs improve the psychological, social, and economic well being of disabled people. One university study found that heart-attack victims were more likely to be alive after a year if they had an animal. Another study suggested that older adults visit the doctor less if they own a dog or cat. Still another study showed that dogs improve morale among nursing-home residents. Two additional studies found that dogs can be great stress buffers. Being with a dog can reduce the effects of stress. It's no wonder that many therapists use dogs to help calm people in therapy.

Service dogs help people with disabilities live full, rich lives. They also keep people with disabilities safe. Therapy dogs can pull people out of despair and can help create emotional healing.

Actress Betty White knows about dogs' power to heal. In her essay "Pet Love," published in *Chicken Soup for the Pet Lover's Soul*," she writes that when her husband died, her first instinct was to crawl away and mourn. But her dogs, Timmy and Sooner, "were not about to let [her] just wither away." Her dogs helped her heal following her loss. She says, "They gave my life definition—a reason to get up in the morning." Betty White is grateful to her dogs for their help. She says that their healing gave her "an unwavering constant . . . a dependable reservoir of comfort and love." No doubt she shares that love with her dogs.

If you have a disability or any physical or mental health challenge, look for ways that your dog, or a dog specifically trained for your problem, can help. You can search online to find information about guide dogs and helping dogs.

It's No Big Deal

The things dogs do to help you heal seem to come naturally to them. They don't sit down and ponder what they can do to help. They just do what feels right at the moment. What's amazing is that what feels right to them is often exactly what you need.

Dog owners who don't seem to know better often exclude their dogs when someone is sick, locking the dog out of a child's sickroom or shoving the dog aside when they have a headache. These people are missing out. They're also making things harder on themselves in the process. They have at their fingertips a cheap and enjoyable healing tool, and they're ignoring it.

Dogs, by their very presence, can help you heal. Dog parents know this. You know that taking care of a dog properly can nudge you to do things that are beneficial to your own health. In the process of caring for yourself, you give your dog a better life. She thrives on being with you. Dogs in general thrive on love. The better you feel, the more you can love. The more your dog is loved, the more she can help you heal. That's a cycle dog parents can happily perpetuate.

A Final Tail Wag

In *The Shaman Bulldog: A Love Story*, Renaldo Fischer writes about his beloved bulldog, Faccia Bello, "My last night with Faccia Bello, I lit some candles and thanked God for the great gift of this companion."

For years, I've kept a gratitude journal. Every night, I write down in the journal five things I have or that I received or experienced during the day for which I'm grateful. It's a ritual I find calming and one that reminds me of life's blessings even on the toughest days.

Every day, when I write down those five things, my dog is the first thing on the list. Always. My dogs have always been one of the greatest blessings in my life.

The writer called SARK points out on her wonderful poster titled, "Dogs Are Miracles with Paws," that "God made dogs and spelled his own name backwards!"

Poet Rainer Maria Rilke wrote, "God . . . sat down for a moment when the dog was finished in order to watch it . . . and to know it was good, that nothing was lacking, that it could not have been better." How *could* the dog be any better? Dogs are pure love. Pure love is unconditional love. Unconditional love is your connection with the divine. Dogs, therefore, are your connection with God or whatever you call the divine spirit in our universe.

Consequently, I believe being a dog parent is a divine calling. Dogs give themselves into your care with nothing but a desire to love and be loyal to you. You can go through the motions of taking care of them, and you can love them when and in ways that are convenient to you. Or you can love them as unconditionally as they love you. That's what being a dog parent is all about.

One final aspect of being a great dog parent is to be always and forever grateful for your dogs' presence in your lives. That gratitude, taking time to thank the divine and your dogs for the gift of their love, reminds you to treat your dogs with appreciation and devotion.

A hug, a pat, a treat, a walk, a toy—these simple things you give your dogs don't come close to matching the love that is in one tail wag. So be grateful for those tail wags. They are one of the greatest joys in life.

WORKS REFERENCED

The Associated Press, "Chiropractor Does Magic—Even If You Have 4 Feet," *Seattle Post-Intelligencer* (December 25, 1998).

Ballner, Maryjean, *Dog Massage* (St. Martin's Press, 2001).

Bergstein, Brian, "The Disabled's Best Friend," *Daily World* (April 3, 1996).

"Bowser the 'Stress Buffer,'" *Your Dog—A Newsletter for Dog Owners* (February 1997).

Burnham, Patricia Gail, *Playtraining Your Dog* (St. Martin's Press, 1980).

Canfield, Jack, et al., *Chicken Soup for the Pet Lover's Soul* (Health Communications, Inc., 1998).

Caras, Roger A., *A Dog Is Listening—The Way Some of Our Closest Friends View Us* (Summit Books, 1992).

Cascade, Kathy, *T Touch—A Unique and Gentle Approach to the Care and Training of Companion Animals,* (brochure).

Coren, Stanley, *How to Speak Dog—Mastering the Art of Dog-Human Communication* (The Free Press, 2000).

Cousins, Norman, *Anatomy of an Illness As Perceived by the Patient* (Bantam Doubleday Dell, 1991).

Cox-Evick, Christina, "Too Busy To Cook—How to Choose the Best Natural Commercial Diet for Your Pet," *Natural Pet Magazine* (January/February 1997).

Dunham, Elisabeth, "Acupuncture and Herbs Debut in Animal Treatment," *News Tribune* (January 12, 1994).

Dworkin, Norine, "Woof! That Feels Good . . . ," *Good Housekeeping* (October 2000).

"Exercise Your Funny Bone," *Vegetarian Times* (June 2001).

Fischer, Renaldo, *The Shaman Bulldog: A Love Story* (Warner Books, Inc., 1996).

Garber, Marjorie, *Dog Love* (Simon & Schuster, 1996).

Gott, Peter H., "Dog's Mouth Full of Germs, but Relax," *Jewish World Review* (November 7, 2000).

Knapp, Caroline, *Pack of Two—The Intricate Bond Between People and Dogs* (Dial Press, 1998).

Masson, Jeffrey Moussaieff, *Dogs Never Lie About Love—Reflections on the Emotional World of Dogs* (Crown Publishers, 1997).

Miller, Stephanie, "Mere Men No Match for Puppy Love," *Bugler* (October 1996).

Morris, Desmond, *Dogwatching—Why Dogs Bark and Everything Else You Ever Wanted to Know* (Crown Publishers, 1986).

Moser, Pat, "Therapist Glad to See Patients Go to the Dog," *News Tribune* (February 11, 1994).

Noonan, Peggy, "New Tricks for Old Cats . . . And Dogs, Too," *USA Weekend* (May 11–13, 2001).

Porterfield, Elaine, "Canine Assistant Knows How to Heal," *News Tribune* (May 11, 1995).

Robinson, Sean, "Pet Ploys—When Owner's Away, Some Cats and Dogs Really Know How to Play," *News Tribune* (April 19, 1998).

Rosen, Michael J., ed., *Dog People—Writers and Artists on Canine Companionship* (Artisan, 1995).

Sheehan, Laurence, *Living with Dogs—Collecting and Traditions, At Home and Afield* (Clarkson Potter Publishers, 1999).

Strombeck, Donald R., *Home-Prepared Dog and Cat Diets—The Healthful Alternative* (Iowa State Press, 1999).

Thomas, Elizabeth Marshall, "Do Animals Have Feelings, Too?", *USA Weekend* (May 10–12, 1996).

Wright, Julie, "Cleanliness Goes to the Dogs," *North Shore News* (November 9, 1998).

INDEX

About the Author

Andrea Rains Waggener is a passionate dog mom. She is also the author of *Healthy, Wealthy, and Wise—Fifty-Two Life-Changing Lessons for the Twenty-First Century* (Hazelden, 2005), *Alternate Beauty* (Bantam, 2005), and *Memories and Murder* (Limitless Dare2Dream, 2006 under pen name Marie Shaw). She writes a newspaper column called "The Up Beat" and publishes an e-newsletter called "Living on the Up Beat," both of which inspire people to live their best lives. She has a B.A. in psychology from The College of William and Mary and a J.D. from Marshall Wythe School of Law, The College of William and Mary. She lives with her husband and her dog on the Washington coast. You, or your dog, can contact Andrea, or Muggins, via her Web site, *www.waggener-books.com.*